Marketing your book

An author's guide

How to target agents,
publishers and readers

Second edition

Alison Baverstock

A & C Black

Second edition 2007

A & C Black Publishers Limited
38 Soho Square
London W1D 3HB
www.acblack.com

First edition published 2001

© 2007, 2001 Alison Baverstock

ISBN: 978–0–7136–7383–8

Typeset in 10/12pt Sabon

Printed and bound in Great Britain

Contents

Acknowledgements   v

Foreword   vii

Introduction   ix

1   The background information that all potential published authors must understand   1

2   What (and why) authors need to know about marketing   16

3   How marketing works in publishing   26

4   Preparing your manuscript for submission   42

5   What to send with your manuscript   52

6   How to find an agent   75

7   Approaching a publisher directly   86

8   Managing without a publisher: when to go it alone   91

9   Working with your publisher   114

10   How to get publicity   129

11   Setting up a website   153

12   Working with booksellers, Amazon and other book retailers   178

13   Literary festivals, working with libraries, reading and writing circles, and other chances to talk about your book   192

14   How to be the perfect speaker   208

15   How to organise a launch event   221

16   Keeping up momentum and morale: before and after publication   234

Index   243

Dedication

For Alasdair, Harriet, Jack and Hamish – still my most fruitful source of market research.

Acknowledgements

Particular thanks are due to Jacqueline Wilson, who manages to become ever-more famous but still has the time to support reading of all kinds, be Children's Laureate, and encourage her many other writing friends. I am very conscious of the support she provides, and am grateful for her new introduction to this book. I would also like to thank Sean McManus and David McClelland, who gave me a crash course in website construction and checked the resulting chapter. Derek Hudson, editor of *Writing Magazine*, assisted this new edition by commissioning me to write a series of articles on the process of submission to agents and publishers. The Society of Authors remains wonderfully supportive to writers, and I find their meetings a particular inspiration. Since early 2006 I have been working with Bloom Partners, who provide a training service for publishers in Australia and New Zealand; this experience, combined with attending the 4th International Conference of the Book in Boston in October 2006, has made me realise that publishers, agents, booksellers and authors are facing the same issues worldwide. I am delighted that many of those I have met and swapped notes with, either physically or in cyberspace, have provided quotations and ideas for the book you are holding.

As usual I consulted many people in my writing, and would particularly like to mention the following:

Clare Alexander, Fiona Allison, Trisha Ashley, Kate Atkinson, Michael Babcock, Jacqueline Banerjee, Victoria Barnsley, Carole Blake, Peter Bolton, Susannah Bowen, Celia Brayfield, Joanna Briscoe, Jenny Brown, Emma Burstall, Helena Caletta, Steven Carey, Linda Carpenter, Harriet Carrow, Catherine Charley, Jane Cholmonley, Genevieve Clarke, Chris Cleave, Julie Cohen, Alain de Botton, Antony Edwards, Shirley Evans, Rachel Feldberg, Katie Fforde, Jane Fisher-Norton, Terrence Frisby, Pauline Goodwin, Jane Gordon-Cumming, Jenny Haddon, Kim Hart, Jo Henry, Gill Hines, Peter Hobday, Deborah Hodges, Heather

Holden-Brown, Dotti Irving, Paul Jeffrey, Catherine Jones, Anna Kiernan, Marte Lavender, Jonnie Leach, Emma Lee-Potter, Mark le Fanu, Catherine Lockerbie, Wendy Lomax, Gian Lombardo, Sally Mays, Peter McCausland, Philippa Milne-Smith, Nicola Morgan, Ed Morrow, Tony Mulliken, Katharine Naish, Chris Perkins, Lakshmi Persaud, Kate Pool, Christine Poulson, Adam Powley, Philip Pullman, Wendy Perriam, Shoo Rayner, Susan Rhodes, Julian Rivers, David Rogers, Stewart Ross, Ben Schott, Liz Small, Nicola Solomon, Charlotte Steer, Linda Strachan, Chantel Sulaiman, Jane Tatam, Simon Trewin, Tony West, Jo and Susan Westwood, Sandy Williams and Chantal Zakari.

Finally I would like to thank my publishers at A&C Black, my agent Jenny Brown, my employers at Kingston University, and my family for a constant stream of new ideas – and challenges.

Foreword

I certainly wasn't an overnight success as a writer. I had my first children's book published when I was 24. For the next 20 years I wrote around 40 books. They all got published – and they mostly sank without trace. How I would have benefited from this brilliant book on marketing in those days!

I got lucky 15 years ago. I was invited to write for the publishers of my dreams. They all work as a team and everyone in the firm is very aware of the importance of clever marketing and publicity. If only all publishers could make this kind of effort for all their authors! But this book offers sound practical advice so that authors can do their best themselves to help make their work successful. We'd all like to think that our books are so beguilingly written with such a strong message that they will whiz up those bestseller charts by merit alone. Sadly it rarely happens that way. The greatest literary work is not much use if there are just a few copies languishing in a warehouse unread. Even the shyest and most retiring of writers want to communicate. They need an audience. Every book needs to be bought.

Alison Baverstock offers sensible useful tips that will help get our books known and appreciated. Authors often grind their teeth and groan about idle or incompetent publishers. She suggests channelling any irritation into positive action. We have to be grown up and take responsibility for our own manuscripts. We might write 'The End' when we've finished each book – but it's only the beginning. Every single author knows the sheer hard work that goes into writing any kind of book. It makes sense to work hard at marketing them too.

In this new edition there's a really helpful chapter on setting up a website. I am a terrible technophobe but even I admit that a good website is invaluable. There's also detailed coverage of literary festivals. Almost every town has its own festival now, and this can be a great way of reaching a whole new audience. It can be nerve-wracking speaking publicly, but I promise that you soon get used to it!

This is a treasury of up-to-date insider information, fascinating anecdotes, and imaginative advice. It will only take a couple of hours to read, but the knowledge gained should last a literary lifetime.

Jacqueline Wilson OBE
Children's Laureate

Introduction

Where was the author of this book when I needed her?

Three years ago I was asked to give a talk to members of the Society of Authors on how authors can market both their books and themselves more effectively. I enjoy giving talks like these. My professional background is in publishing, and although I have now been an author for several years (and had not long before the talk in question written the first edition of this book), I still enjoy explaining to authors how to understand publishing companies and agents, in the same way that the presenters on nature programmes display species that have unusual socio-organisational patterns and are not otherwise encountered.

Just before I was due to go, the phone rang. It was a close friend who works in psychotherapy, in a hospital that, having long been famous for its excellence, had just been cloned twice, with two similar institutions being built – one in Birmingham and a second in Crewe. Now, with both open for just a matter of months, they were threatened with closure. Never mind the investment of time and money involved, and the high hopes riding on these institutions, or the patients now installed and receiving treatment. Whom, she asked, did I know that she and her fellow health professionals could lobby?

I reeled off a couple of names without thinking. Our local MP, Ed Davey, is a strong supporter of mental health issues, feeling that both patients and doctors in this area are under-funded and highly deserving. I mentioned another MP my husband and I were at university with, and gave a couple more influential names (a managing director and a member of the aristocracy), and then thought of a few journalists whom I thought might be interested. I then picked up my briefcase and headed for the train.

Twenty minutes later, installed in my train carriage and gazing out of the window (one of my favourite places to be), I reflected. None of the people whose names I had passed on so freely had any idea that I write. Although officially an author, and at that stage of nine titles, I had never sent any one of them a book, or tried to prompt word of mouth through the organisations they are part of. I write about marketing in publishing; I have a working – or at least revivable – relationship with these people. So why did they not know about what I do?

For most authors it's so much easier if the product is someone else. My first book was written with Jane Austen-like privacy. (If anyone reading this has not been to the cottage at Chawton in Hampshire, and seen the table under whose blotter she would write, a squeaking door announcing the arrival of visitors and the need to put her writing away, it's well worth taking a trip.) I was living in Germany having left my job, and whilst writing a handout for a course I was asked to present, it suddenly struck me that there might be a market for a book telling people beginning as book marketers, as I had been eight years before, how to do their job. I ran the idea past a friend, whose response was negative; submitted it to a publishing house who liked it; remained mute when it was commissioned; and delivered the manuscript four days ahead of my deadline (the day my daughter was due and indeed arrived). And still I told no one – because I had spotted in the contract that publication was likely only if the publishers deemed what I had written 'acceptable'. Only my husband knew. I kept my sweet secret; I sat next to people at dinner parties who told me about their writing ambitions, without ever saying 'well actually, I have just written a book'. Pathetic really – and hugely ironic, considering the subject area I write about.

The transition from being 'published' to being 'a writer' is not automatic; you have to learn to take yourself seriously, and many of us still find that difficult. Most authors are filled with self-doubt: can I ever do it again? Would anyone want to know? We combine a curious mixture of feeling confident in what we have written with an anger that it's not more widely known. Most writers want to communicate and be read, and whilst there is a new breed of authors who see active promotion of themselves and their writing as part of what they do, there are vastly more who combine a desire to communicate with a real disdain for the media that may review them.

And when it comes to promoting ourselves in public, many authors have real difficulty. Firstly there is the illogicality of being asked to get involved in the first place. Why should someone who can string sentences together in print be comfortable doing so in front of a microphone? Why should authors have to turn strumpet and strut their stuff in front of a critical world? And why should those who are comfortable doing these things, and have taken the handy precaution of being surgically enhanced to make them even more photogenic (or not), be awarded contracts for doing something they have never demonstrated any talent for: writing?

Help is at hand. This book is packed with advice on how to get your book noticed, ensure that you yourself are taken seriously as an author, and build relationships with everyone: agents, publishers, readers and recommenders. The advice in these pages is not rocket science. I have tried not to overburden you with information on how the industry works, but there are things that writers really do need to know if they are to help their books along. So whether you bought this book to help you get a contract with an agent or publishing house, or to improve sales from the books you already have in print, I hope it will assist.

The observant reader will notice endless references to Kingston-upon-Thames and its environs. This is not (as those outside the M25 may hastily conclude) because I think the south of England best or, even worse, because I am parochial. My parents were from the Midlands; I was born in Suffolk, grew up in Shropshire and Hertfordshire and went to university in Scotland. Since then I have lived all over the place due to my husband's itinerant job (one publicity manager claimed that mine was the longest 'local press' list on an author publicity form that she had ever seen). Some of the best bits of this book were written whilst I was attending the 4th International Conference of the Book in Boston, USA. So whilst I am devoted to Kingston, and it's wonderful to finally feel settled, my knowledge of bookshops and other goings-on in my home area is also pragmatic. Authors do well to cultivate their own acre of ground; their local bookshops, literary festivals, associations, libraries and so on.

Finally, I hope too that the book will boost a wider consideration for the author. Many now think of writing as a swift path to riches; something that can be achieved between lunch and tea on a series of wet Wednesdays. The reality is so different. The craft of writing demands long hours, is poorly paid and generally put down. Hence we need to offer each other encouragement, especially when doing something we do not feel comfortable with – which may include self-marketing.

Alison Baverstock
June 2007

1

The background information that all potential published authors must understand

Two of the words in the title of this book are not natural bed-fellows. I refer to *marketing* and *author*.

Marketing as a term is becoming more acceptable all the time. New generations of students happily enrol on university courses that bear its name, convinced that an understanding of the subject is key to their future employability, and the wholehearted embracing of marketing by political parties has convinced many otherwise scep-tical individuals that attempting to communicate with your market, and persuade them to your point of view, can be highly effective. But whilst the onward march of marketing's impact is beyond doubt, there is still at least an association in the public mind between 'marketing' and the foisting of goods and services that are not really required onto the gullible and unsuspecting; a lingering perception that if things were any good, they would sell on their own.

This is partly culturally specific. British society is notoriously conservative about selling things – hence the attempts to disguise the 's' word in job titles, such as 'information manager/executive/ customer-facing staff', rather than saying that they work in sales; certainly this is the case in comparison with North America. But how much marketing is desirable, is also an issue that applies with particular force in the selling of cultural commodities. Should individual voices and viewpoints *need* to be marketed, rather than simply be noticed for their own intrinsic merit? Don't most of us harbour a nostalgia for the writer or musician whose work we enjoyed in isolation, or the companionship of a few other insight-ful cognoscenti, before they became 'popular'?

The term *author* is similarly loaded; it's seen as a calling rather than a job, and a term that many writers are reluctant to apply to themselves too soon, for fear of risking bad luck or ridicule. Many writers keep their calling to themselves until they have reached a certain point of success. Scribes producing words for advertising campaigns tend to call themselves 'writers', or 'copywriters', and journalists refer to themselves as such, or as 'hacks'. Somehow being an *author* is perceived as (or is, given that the author is usually required to produce more words for each selling unit) a slightly higher calling, requiring more devotion to the writing art, and certainly years of rejection, low income, commiseration and patronage (whether in resources or in attitude) from friends and colleagues.

Hence the awkward collision of these two words in the area of *author marketing*, the subject of this book. A large number of authors find it distasteful. They want to write – not to have to talk up their book or do book tours or signing sessions, at which they feel uncomfortable and risk humiliation. Why, after all, should those who communicate through words on a page necessarily be articulate when placed in front of a microphone or large crowds? This is a completely different skill. Many writers feel awkward with the very concept of marketing, and believe that attempts to sell (or popularise) their ideas compromise their artistic integrity. Their work should be appreciated on its merits rather than be tweaked to suit the needs of commercial marketing plans that feel artificially imposed, or of an increasingly fickle market. Few writers find that they can support themselves by their writing straight away, and so must juggle jobs. This is easier in some fields than others. Within academia, for example, whilst a determination to share learning can be seen as an ethical responsibility of the teacher, based on Christian ethics ('To whom much has been given, much will be expected' [Luke 12; 48]), ironically the desire to communicate can be seen as a vulgar seeking of popularity that is incompatible with academic status. Alain de Botton has written that '…hostility to anyone attempting to communicate ideas to a broader public is a staple of academic life. You can either fight for academic status or you can address the world at large. But in the current British climate it's very difficult to succeed in both fields.'[1]

1 *Times* Magazine, 26th August 2006

Whilst I understand the reluctance on the part of authors to get involved in the marketing of what they write, increasingly those who distance themselves from the selling process place themselves and their work at a disadvantage. Publishing decisions about whether or not to take on specific new authors are made at regular meetings, and the most commonly used word when discussing them is 'promoteable'; an author's willingness and enthusiasm for getting involved in the process does make a difference. It does not replace the need for a good manuscript or writing idea, but it does help – whatever is being written about. In some areas, the author's saleability matters more than their ability to write; when commissioning a celebrity biography, for example, the skill is in selecting a ghost-writer who can create the voice of someone the public genuinely wants to hear from. In defence of publishers, whilst some writers may react negatively to this information, it is true that the market place is very crowded today. Potential customers have a much wider range of choice of entertainment than was available to their parents' generation, and the contribution made by the author is often crucial in getting books noticed:

'I think there is a real tendency to think, "Once I get published, I've done it," and then you watch your book go nowhere. You can't just be a writer – you've got to be your own cheerleader.'

Jodi Picoult, interviewed in *The Telegraph Magazine*, 2nd September 2006

Significantly, this is nothing new:

'Every great and original writer, in proportion as he is great and original, must himself create the taste by which he is to be relished.'

William Wordsworth (1770–1850)

What this book is for

This book explains what marketing is – how it works in general, and its particular application within publishing – and provides guidelines on how to market your own work, whether to an agent or publisher before publication, or to the wider reading public afterwards. It's important to understand that *purchase (or reading) of this book does not replace the need to produce a well-crafted and readable book*, of whatever sort you are planning. It simply helps you to present your writing with the best chance of positive attention from those who are making key decisions about whether or not they should publish or read you.

Why I am writing this book

This is a second edition of a title that did well when first published five years ago. Since first publication, however, a number of important things have changed, and new opportunities arisen. For example, it now costs vastly less for authors to create and maintain their own websites, and there has been a huge rise in the number of reading and writing festivals. Both of these increase the market for books, and create more competition to get published. A new edition was called for.

In the meantime, I had published this book's prequel – a serious look at the resources you need if you are going to get a book published. Called *Is there a book in you?*, it came out in July 2006 (also from A&C Black). The book you are holding now follows on from where that title left off. It makes an assumption that if you are reading this, you are serious about trying to get your work published; that you have something ready (even if unfinished) to show publishers and agents; and that you feel compelled to continue with your work. In other words, it assumes that you *really* do want to get published. It will give advice on how to format, whom to approach and what to send. The guidelines included here will also be of great assistance if you have already published a book or books, and want to help your work get wider attention – whether from your agent, publisher, bookseller or the reading public.

I feel qualified to write this book because, as an author and publisher, I have been on both sides of the fence. I left university for the publishing industry, and worked in marketing on all kinds of published products, from high-level journals to educational books, from novels to children's titles. And whilst I now mostly write, I still work freelance within the industry, offering training and consultancy. I have seen how particular authors help or hinder their chances of getting published because of their attitude and/or the way they behave. I have seen how authors' careers as promoted writers are affected by their own pro-activity and ideas, both positively and negatively.

I have been the publisher who wishes that authors would consolidate their requests into a single communication, rather than interrupt my working day with sequential phone calls: most authors have little understanding that there are books other than their own which need attention. But I have also been the author, feeling isolated at home and wondering if anyone really cares about my book apart from me. I have asked myself if publishers really appreciate just how hard it is to keep going as a writer, and how deflating their lack of apparent interest can be.

The approach I offer in this book is pragmatic and informed. I don't expect you to turn overnight into a 24/7 savvy provider of media-friendly sound-bites; rather, I aim to help you understand how books get noticed, and to equip you to use the media that offer the most positive opportunities for the wider promotion of your particular talents. My hope is that once provided with the information in this book, you will be better able to present your writing idea, in its most attractive form, to those with a serious interest in representing, publishing or reading it.

How trying to get a book published feels

Trying to get a book published is like:

*   Attempting to get your child into an over-subscribed school. You worry and find yourself wondering what are the odds on success; how can you best improve their chances; what are other people up to? And the answer for some is pretty desperate, like moving house (and 'downsizing' to get into the right postcode); signing up for coaching at a very early age; providing a false address that does fall within the magic postcode area; dreaming up the 'special circumstances' that provide a shortcut to the top of the list. Anything to achieve that desired goal.

- Trying to get pregnant when it does not happen as quickly as you would like. Similarly, being approved as adoptive parents and then each month scanning the relevant publications to find a likely youngster, and then starting the process of asking for your papers to be forwarded to the relevant social worker. You spend the month in a state of anxiety and then it starts all over again.

- Applying for a new job. Presenting yourself as positively as possible; trying to make the right impression at the interview and then waiting for the outcome.

- Wanting to move house, and finding that new properties are in short supply, and so having to continually chase estate agents to send you information on properties that are interesting to you, before they inform your friends and neighbours, who are also planning to move. And then the angst that follows as you have your offer accepted but fear that the other party may pull out (unless you are reading this in Scotland).

- Standing on the starting line for a race – perhaps even that most competitive event, the fathers' race at school sports day.

- Going into an open competition exam with your examination number ready to write down, with perhaps an associated fear that you might have left an incriminating piece of paper in your pocket (which would bring an accusation of 'academic misconduct').

If the thought of any of these situations gets the adrenaline pumping inside you, then you begin to understand how trying to get published will feel. But there is a crucial difference. In all the situations mentioned, you are aware of your rights as a consumer, patient or citizen. There are clear positions in law that entitle you to be heard/seen/have your views considered, even if you are ultimately deemed time-wasting, wrong, or fraudulent; you may not care what those you are dealing with think of you. When you are trying to get a book published you have all of the same longings, but none of the same rights. You must remain pleasant, and not give them a clue that you might turn difficult after a decision to commission you. And of course the ultimate difference is that you are doing this to yourself; you don't have to take part – and a large proportion of your acquaintance and family will conclude that you are foolish even to try.

Grasping the essentials: the two opposing camps, who must work together if you are to publish a book

The subheading uses adversarial language – surely publishers and authors should be united in their desire to produce a good and widely read book? Why the reference to 'sides' and 'opposition'?

Anyone who tries to get published will quickly understand that there are two main groups of people involved in the process: publishers (and I would include agents here, as they are part of the same system), and authors – and that frequently, it feels like a situation of 'us' and 'them'. Gather any group of authors together and they will moan about their publishers – most usually about the lack of marketing for their books. Attend the London (or indeed any) book fair, and the authors, whose works form the main body of what is being bartered and sold on such occasions, are present only in picture form, like the sanitised mantlepiece of an elderly aunt who finds the images of her unruly relatives easier to deal with than their boisterous presence.

The views of publishers and authors about each other are often polarised. They need each other and cannot survive effectively without each other, but the problem for writers (potential and actual) is that *it's a buyers' market*; there are vastly more people wanting to get published than have the talent to make it, than there are production resources within the industry to put into print, or shelf space in shops to stock.

Authors often complain that publishers lack an appreciation of how what they provide is the basis of the industry they feed. They feel marginalised by publishers who have no real understanding of how much effort it takes to write a book, all the while conscious that their ability to do so again is not automatic – whereas publishers blithely assume that it is infinitely sustainable.

Without authors there can be no publishing industry, and yet still one gets the impression, whenever publishers are gathered together, that this is a party to which authors are not really invited; they would get on faster without them – and write the wretched books themselves if only they had the time.

For the first edition of this book I collected a series of authors' gripes about the industry, each one a tale of mean spirit, grudge or just lack of awareness of the potential of their major suppliers. The chapter was printed as an extract in *The Bookseller* magazine and caused a great cheer amongst authors, and a bit of a stir within the publishing industry. But even in discussing the reaction, the publishers somehow missed the point. *The Bookseller* editorial, which discussed the issue I had raised in the same edition, commented that it should be of concern to the industry that many authors 'whose work is central to the publishing process, feel alienated from it'.

Frankly this reaction annoyed authors even more. Most feel they are not 'central to a process', but rather that the 'process' would not exist without them. We do not have a 'process of publishing' as an independent good, like a constitutional monarchy or democratically elected government. You do not search for authors as a commodity in the same way that you indent for chairs or paperclips; rather the role of the writer, the person who comes up with the ideas, is crucial. In any case, most authors would feel that the publishers seldom have to go searching, in the way that a production director would seek out new materials. What they have to do is recognise the merit of what has already been offered to them, sent to their doors, with return postage supplied.

> 'I don't believe that it's the writer's job to respond to some vague idea about what readers want. Readers don't know what they want until they see what you can offer. Nowadays, we're told, they're all asking for the next Harry Potter, but no-one ever asked for the first Harry Potter. It took JK Rowling to think of him before people realised that this was something they might like to read. The writer and the idea always come first, and are always the most important thing.'
> Philip Pullman

It's true today that many 'published' authors have not actually written the books (celebrity biographies are a notable example), but it is still the 'author' – or name on the cover – that draws the interest. Interestingly this often catches publishers by surprise, when figures such as Sharon Osborne and Katie Price (aka

Jordan) go on to be huge bestsellers, simply because people are fascinated by their lives.

The things authors dislike about publishers

Publishers do not understand how hard writing is
Authors often complain that publishers have no idea how difficult it is to write a book. They don't know how long it takes, how lonely is the process, how much – once it is over – you worry about ever being able to do it again. Authors can't tell publishers just how much they want to be published; the extent to which rushed decisions made in meetings affect their aspirations and lives; how spur-of-the-moment phone calls, when they sound keen one minute and full of doubt the next, can play with authors' hopes and desires. Contact with publishers is exhausting: you can swing from optimism to pessimism, and all before 11.00 in the morning.

All this uncertainty is further complicated by the fact that publishers frequently seem to have their own writing ambitions. Authors worry that this may impede their judgement of other people's writing talent: because they are so often thinking 'that's not the way I'd write it', their instincts get in the way of spotting stories that other people want to read.

Publishers are not effective communicators
To be frank, many publishers are not good at communicating with authors (or even each other). Ring a branch of your building society, and via the 'security questions' that follow, the call-handler ensures that it is you calling; he or she then has access to a screen of information about you, giving all the details of your previous relationship (you can tell because they try to read it before talking to you – 'can you just bear with me for a minute'). More information will be added during each conversation, and it will all be available to the next person who takes a call from you.

Publishers don't work like this. Information that you send to your editorial contact will not necessarily be passed on to the sales department, who could benefit from it too. The information stream is poor the other way: lots of things that the author might like to know – how many books are being printed; where and when; how they are selling? – are simply not communicated. Some speculate that authors are kept in ignorance in order to prevent them from interfering in future/trying to negotiate a better deal.

Over the whole area of marketing, which might seem an obvious area of overlap between publishers and authors, some houses give the distinct impression that they would rather authors did not get involved, and left everything to them. Whilst they have the history, and no doubt a range of set procedures, leaving it all to them is a big risk to take.

> 'I do think (and you can quote me on this) that it's *remarkable* how much authors can achieve, sometimes by working with their publisher, but sometimes just by doing it anyway. A publisher's knowledge about what *normally* works can blind them to what *might* work, and the author's naïvete and "ignorance" can actually be a boon, because we sometimes come up with off-the-wall ideas which *can* work. Of course, we have to make sure that what we do doesn't interfere with what the publisher is doing – but some publishers fear that too much. I think the ideal situation is when the author and the publisher recognise each other's values and strengths.'
>
> Nicola Morgan, children's author

Publishers keep changing jobs

During the lifetime of a book, authors will find themselves dealing with many different people. Of course the different functions require different people, but within each role, changes of personnel seem to be very frequent. There are notable exceptions (the first edition of this book appeared five years ago and I'm delighted to say that the same team are in place this time around), but publishers tend to job-hop a lot. This can be a devastating experience for a writer: just as you find someone who really likes your work, they move on and the next incumbent is not so keen, leaving you feeling orphaned.

Publishing is not well organised

To authors, publishing often seems like a randomly operated business: working low margins; launching too many new titles;

making gimmicky and speculative approaches to markets rather than planning sustained campaigns – publishing can look gloriously amateur. In their defence, it's very hard to predict the reading taste of the public, and the most unlikely titles become best-sellers. And because the products have low prices (around £7.99 for a paperback novel, £14.99 for a hardback), and sell in relatively low numbers, marketing budgets tend to be low too – hence the pursuit of free publicity through the media.

Publishing has never paid well, and has traditionally attracted lots of well-brought-up young ladies who were thus respectably occupied until marriage. Whilst this is no longer universally true – and there have been a number of initiatives aimed at widening entry – the workforce remains predominantly white, middle-class and well spoken. This can lead to real confusion – authors who feel that they are being encouraged are in fact being given a polite brush-off. Authors also complain that publishers do not understand the wider markets to which their limited life experience does not expose them. But publishers have full-time jobs, and authors who work from home have more opportunity to experience and explore daily life in all sorts of different ways. One could conclude that it is up to them to educate publishers about markets that would respond well to their writing, rather than berating them for not knowing about them already.

Publishers have big egos
See below.

Things not to say to a publisher

I've always wanted to write a book.
Even if I don't get published I'll still carry on writing.
I've tried everyone else.
Such and such a firm said there was no room on their list just now, so I hope it might suit you ...
I invite you to peruse[2] the chapters I enclose.
I sued my last publisher/was involved in a lawsuit.

2 All publishers seem to hate this word

The things that publishers dislike about authors

Authors fail to appreciate that publishing is a profession, and effective publishing is the product of experience

Stories of manuscripts picked up from the slush pile are motivating, but they stand out because they are rare; publishers get it right more often than they get it wrong. Authors persistently underestimate their professionalism.

There are authors who think that all the publisher has to do is press a few buttons, wait for the books to be delivered and then count the takings. This is a gross misrepresentation of how much care and skill is involved. Pitching a book to a market, preparing a manuscript that is fit for publication, planning how the book should look and feel, commissioning a cover and preparing the cover blurb that will make it appeal to the market in question, all take time and experience. In any case, it's not always the author who comes up with the idea for the book – it's not uncommon for the publisher to have an idea, draft a contents list, choose someone to write it, propose the idea in-house and create enthusiasm for it, rewrite what is submitted as it is not up to the required standard ... and then watch the 'author' take full credit. Successful publishers must often bite their tongue.

Authors are self-obsessed

Publishers are inclined to view some authors as over-indulged children: attention-seeking, neurotic and narcissistic. Over the years, I've given many talks on self-marketing to groups of authors, and whilst the majority of the audience are pleasant, the stereotype definitely exists. Publishers are wary.

Of course each author is producing their own books, but the publishing house has the rest of their list to be concerned with. An accusation that authors think only of their book, and not of the rest of the output, is a common one.

Authors are unrealistic and too demanding

Just because an idea occurs does not mean it is a good one. Not every idea thought up by an author is automatically printable.

There are authors who view the industry as a branch of the NHS, from which they are somehow entitled to receive attention and production, irrespective of the merits – or saleability – of their manuscript (and they don't want to be told that it's unpublishable). Not every book can land the author an interview with Richard and Judy or Parkinson.

Authors are rude
There are authors who demand the earth, but never bother to comment on anything that goes well. Failing to thank for a launch party, or any extra effort by the publishing house, such as getting books to an event that the author only informed them was happening at the last minute, is particularly annoying.

Authors are needy
A writer's life is like a rollercoaster. The difficulty is that most authors want publication so much: it's something they have worked towards, in incremental degrees, through writing for parish newsletters and local papers, until at last, the goal of a book in print appears like a mirage before them. It's difficult to be strategic and objective when you want something so desperately; every word a publisher utters will be dwelt upon later, dissected and examined for wider meaning. Is this proof of author neediness, or just evidence of their enormous desire for what publishers can offer?

Authors can be unhelpful
Marketing in publishing often relies on a search for free publicity, and because opportunities may occur at the last minute, you may get asked questions you have been asked before. Responding with 'I have already told your editorial director, I suggest you ask him' is not helpful, particularly if the latter is away and the information is needed urgently. And if someone has had a bad experience talking to you, it's an opportunity that may not come again.

Similarly, the marketing department of a publishing house is seldom on stand-by waiting to leap into action once they hear from an author. The workload has to be juggled. Leaflets can't always be provided at the last minute, but with enough warning they can be produced. Remain in touch about what you are up to;

you can't assume that your publisher knows all the details of your professional life since you last filled in an Author Publicity form.

So if you are giving a talk, or you want information sent to a conference where you are giving a paper, provide all the right details. Don't assume that the initials you know it by, and the precise location in Boston, are known by your publisher – even though they are engrained in *your* psyche, and being asked to speak is the greatest thing that has happened to you since 1980.

Authors have big egos
See below.

Things not to say to an author

I'll give you a ring to talk about this sometime. No, I can't say when I'll ring, but I'm sure I'll catch you in …
It's a good idea, but you're not famous enough.
There's no enthusiasm for this idea in-house.
Just rework this; it won't take you long.
I know I said I would ring, but I was busy.
I've got this great idea for a novel.
I like the idea in principle, but can you rewrite the novel from the point of view of a 12-year-old boy?

Achieving a resolution – understanding the ego issue

I raised the issue of ego, but confusingly have placed it as an item for consideration by both parties – because both accuse each other of over-egotism. This has always seemed ironic to me, as egos survive, indeed thrive, on both sides of the publishing fence. It's a creative industry.

It's impossible to write a book without having a strong ego; the idea of assuming that your thoughts and experiences are interesting to the wider population is an act of great egotism. But remember that ego as originally outlined by Freud was good – and without its existence in authors, there would be no books.

Publishers can be equally egotistical. The confidence with which they feel able to deflate authors' writing ideas, even when they are in the most junior positions or lack even a basic understanding of the market being approached, is certainly evidence of an egotistical belief in their own powers of judgement – although often it seems more like breathtaking arrogance.

Authors are keen to promote their own book, failing (either deliberately or unconsciously) to consider the other titles a publishing house may be handling over the same period.

Publishers tend to assume a much wider level of information (and indeed interest) amongst the reading public about their organisations than is the case; most people know the names of their favourite writers but have little idea who publishes them. Individual house imprints (e.g. Viking, Vintage, Abacus) are even less well known. Watch any group of publishers in action and you will observe a scene worthy of the attention of David Attenborough: the strutters and the stalkers; those who wander around with an immense awareness of their own talent, general attractiveness and the vital part they play in bringing reading material to the washed masses (they are, for the most part, less interested in the unwashed).

Both publishers and authors tend to assume that many more people want to read than actually do, and they are fond of adding a moralistic value to what they *should* be doing with their time.

Summary of this chapter

There is an entirely symbiotic relationship between authors and publishers. They need each other, and understanding the perceptions and expectations of both sides is vital. This book is here to help you do just that: to explain how publishing works, to enable you to market your book – whether to an agent or to a publisher – and then, once you are published, to help you market your work to your readers.

2

What (and why) authors need to know about marketing

I'm a firm believer in definitions. If you define precisely what you are talking about, then you have more chance of both setting realistic objectives and achieving your aims.

Nowhere is this more important than in marketing. Marketing often presents an image of chaotic flurry: too much money being spent in an apparently random pursuit of the unattainable. But true marketing is the calculated application of resources where they are most likely to yield effect.

So, we will start with an understanding of marketing theory and then proceed with a description of how this relates to the promotion of books.

Definitions of marketing are particularly problematic. Academics cannot agree, and many articles have been written about what marketing means. And perhaps because marketing is a relatively new discipline for academic study, it has been over-afflicted by 'verbiage' – the desire of those working in the subject to provide an appropriate (and some would say impenetrable) vocabulary to elevate the subject. It seems to me that relatively new academic disciplines such as sociology, art history and marketing are much more prone to this than are more established subjects, such as history and English.

Equally unhelpful are the demotic – but far more memorable – terms associated with marketing via the media: 'hoodwinked', 'conned', 'suckered', 'landed with', as well as the range of consumer interest programmes conveying the basic message that anyone selling anything is most likely trying to rob or con you. It is certainly true that many authors feel a genuine distaste for the commercial, and an even greater disdain for the associated language. Even if you too have little liking for marketing and marketing-speak, try to remember the following:

1 Most people enjoy spending money.
It's quite common to see purchasing described as 'retail therapy'. As journalist Ruth Picardie wrote, when dying of cancer:

> 'Essentially, after months of careful research, I have discovered a treatment that is a) cheaper than complementary therapy b) a hell of a lot more fun than chemotherapy and c) most important, incredibly effective! Retail therapy! ... Thanks to this highly evolved, only moderately expensive and largely side-effect free treatment, I am currently in almost no pain! ... My non-beard book, *Shop Yourself out of Cancer*, is coming soon.'[1]

2 Books are very reasonably priced.
For the would-be book-buyer, the financial entry point is low and the purchase could be the start of a long-term relationship. Even those who buy a book that they subsequently find they hate emerge with that most useful of social assets: an opinion.

A very basic definition of marketing

Marketing means effective selling: making your sales proposal to the market so appealing that a decision to purchase is the result.

Obviously the definition will vary according to whether it is a product, service or information that you are making available, and the response you want from the market (purchase, decision, recommendation, donation, and so on). But this basic definition will serve us very well. For the author, it is helpful to think of marketing in terms of making the potential market for a book aware of the product and then encouraging them to purchase.

Now let's break down this definition further and pull out various threads of argument. There are several useful checklists for doing so – you may well be familiar with the formula of Ps:

1 *Before I Say Goodbye*, Ruth Picardie, Penguin 1998

people, product, promotion, place, price, personnel, and so on. I would like to offer the following subheadings; the first four are courtesy of Professor Baker of Strathclyde University, and the last two are my own.

Marketing means focusing on the customer

This is the one thing everyone does agree on. Every marketing definition I have ever seen mentions the word 'customer'.

So, thinking about this from the author's point of view, what kind of people buy your books and why? Don't assume that they are all like you. I heard Margaret Atwood recently describe her readers as hugely diverse, defying any group categorisation, and that this had been realised through her very large and varied postbag. She summed them up as 'Dear Reader'.

If your titles are aimed at a specific market (for example, educational or professional) then categorising your readers becomes much easier, but there is still a range of questions that you should be asking yourself. (And it *is* you who should be doing the asking, rather than the publisher; your overall market knowledge will be better than theirs.)

- At what stage in their professional career will they benefit from your book?
- How will they use it? What needs (current or future) will it meet?
- What job title do they have? This will probably need several variants – try to provide them all.
- What professional associations do they belong to and how often do they meet up? Can you source the relevant lists of members?

Marketing needs a long perspective

Effective marketing cannot be achieved overnight. It takes detailed thought, and thought takes time.

If your publisher were to double the amount spent on marketing your titles tomorrow, you would probably not see the effect on sales by next week. It might even produce the opposite effect, as spending too much money on a promotion can alienate a market. For example, imagine making a decision to increase the production specification (in other words, improve the overall quality of the materials being used) for a mailshot appealing for money for starving children. The most likely result would be to repel the market; it would look as if too much had been spent on production, and therefore less had reached the children in need.

Along the same lines, think about how long a promotion piece is going to be around for and whether contemporary events referred to in the leaflet will date or change in how they are perceived. In addition, watch out for words that, although currently popular, are likely to date, and in particular those words that are used by politicians to describe new initiatives. If your material must last a long time, the words must too.

Effective marketing means using all the resources at your disposal

Effective marketing means using all the resources of a company to promote sales, not just those of one department. In practice, this means that the various departments within a publishing house should be communicating and working towards the same end.

Certain publishing houses are known to produce particular kinds of books. Thus, simply saying that a poetry title comes from Bloodaxe, or a music-teaching title from A&C Black, means that it will get greater respect from the market and those reviewing it than would be the case if they had never heard of the publisher.

If you become aware that a publishing house is not particularly efficient at internal communication, then you will have to work doubly hard to ensure that the information you send in is seen by all who need access to it – it's probably best to send two copies!

Marketing means being both innovative and flexible

This is true of marketing in all fields. We tire quickly and are eager for the new and different. Some of the recent marketing successes flew in the face of conventional wisdom: for example, initial market research on the Sony Walkman was not positive, as the benefits of a tape recorder into which you could not record were not seen.

Some of publishing's big successes in recent years have been as much of a surprise to the publishing house as to the public. The books of Bill Bryson, Joanne Harris and JK Rowling all began as relatively low-budget promotions; they caught the reading public's imagination and the rest, as they say, is history.

It is also important to keep track of what else consumers spend their money on, and how these products are marketed. So start reading your direct mail, ask people you meet what they think of bookshops and what makes them pick up new titles, and read advertisements for products in the street. I find my children an endlessly fertile source of market research.

Marketing depends on relationships

This seems to me a point of fundamental importance. Effective marketing builds up relationships between all those you wish to include: shareholders, purchasers, existing and potential employees.

This point seems to me to apply with particular force in publishing. The relationship between reader and writer lasts a long time, as the book is read, remembered, and usually kept. And the deeper the experience inspired by the book (whether positive or negative), the truer this is.

Writers report that the letters, and increasingly emails, they receive from readers can be extremely perceptive, and website-chatrooms also attest to the involvement felt – some raising copyright issues when ideas develop so far from the original creator. Those who write to authors, and receive a satisfactory answer, enthuse wider, and so your audience grows.

The same goes for relationships with publishing houses. For example, I remember when the Virago books first appeared. I loved the books themselves (Rosamund Lehmann and Radclyffe Hall were two authors I discovered this way) and also the format – the rich green, largish print and beautiful cover images. Virago published authors who were out of print and forgotten, and I bought many. They then seemed to start publishing books which, although still beautifully packaged, were perhaps deservedly out of print. I lost confidence and, after a couple of unenjoyable reads, never bought a Virago paperback again. This was not a vindictive decision, and not something I realised until years later. It was just that my confidence was dented and I started to look elsewhere – so other authors undoubtedly benefited from my change of allegiance.

Lastly, remember that relationships do not have to be good to be remembered. Memories in the book business can be very long, as those who have had negative reviews of their books will be aware.

Marketing is logical
This means you need to think about what you are trying to achieve and then attempt to realise your goals. Planning is essential – and so is being informed.

As you become involved with a publishing house you enter a world of new words and formats. You may be confused about the range of promotional materials that publishing houses produce, but in Chapter 3 I describe each of these, and the logic behind them, so that if asked to contribute to or comment on the copy[2] you understand why it is being created.

Particular problems confronted by those selling books

Many would rather do something else than read
As authors, we are committed to thinking that books are wonderful. Whilst there are many who agree with us, sadly there are even more who find the book irrelevant:

> 'I don't really read books: there's not enough space in my life. When I have an empty space in my brain, it's cool, it's OK. I don't want to fill it with anything.'
>
> Celine Dion, singer, *Sunday Times Magazine*, October 1999

Books have to compete with a vast range of other items that cost about the same – or perhaps more – but take less decision-making time. Nor is one book always competing with another title for the customer's money. An alternative to buying a book could be a training course (costing vastly more) or a meal out; the customer is not necessarily deciding between two books.

2 Descriptive words

Others see books as worthy, boring necessities

Generations of schoolchildren have grown up with a view of books as boring necessities associated with homework. The dilapidated condition of the book stock in schools, and poor access (class sets often consist of one between two rather than one each) have compounded this problem.

There are definite ways in which the author can help here. Subheadings encourage the reader to get involved, as do page layouts that reflect modern design – for example with boxes, highlighted quotes and 'sound-bites'. A study of magazine layout will yield further examples.

Book purchase takes ages

Choosing a book demands a great investment of time – and this is true whether one is a buyer in a bookshop, or a consumer trying to choose between the titles they have selected. And the time one has to invest – to read the blurb, look at the cover, perhaps read the first paragraph, look at the index, and so on – is in inverse proportion to the financial investment required, as most books sell for a relatively low purchase price.

> 'Choosing a new item of clothing can take me seconds: do I like the colour, is my size available, is it machine washable? Ironically, the final purchase price can be ten times that of a paperback book that it takes me ten times longer to choose.'
>
> Waterstone's customer

> 'I realised that the amount of time I invested in each customer – getting to know them; building a relationship; recommending titles they might like and ordering what I did not have in stock – was probably yielding about 20p per title sold. As I was running my bookshop as a business and not, as many of my customers assumed, as a hobby, this was hardly a cost-effective way of making a living.'
>
> Recently retired independent bookseller

How can the author help guide the reader to what they want to know quickly? By providing concise and interesting information on both the book and yourself whenever possible! The following was drafted as advice for talking to reporters, but is equally relevant to any form of author information. In *Managing the Message*, former *Today Programme* presenter Peter Hobday commented:

> 'It never ceases to amaze me the amount of useless personal information an individual will give a reporter – about the committees they serve on, whether they are chairman, treasurer or secretary, how many clubs they belong to. The very grandest will airily hand you a photocopy of their entry in *Who's Who*. It is far better that you, rather than the reporter, should decide what you think is relevant. From your obviously glittering and lengthy CV choose the few – very few or better still no more than two – facts that seem to be most germane to the interview in hand. The object of the exercise is to make sure that you are seen as the right person to be talking about this issue.'

Customers only buy the same book once

If you decide you like a particular brand of chocolate, or spirit, you will go on buying the same brand until you change your mind, which may be never. Publishers seldom have the same opportunity. There are occasions when a title is bought again, for example as a present, but these are relatively rare. Each book is a different product; hence the desire of publishing houses to build a brand to represent a particular type of author or house. That is why your book may end up looking relatively similar to others in the same genre (group of related titles, e.g. thrillers or romantic fiction to be sold through supermarkets).

The publisher can never be sure when books are sold

Because of the number of titles available, and the importance of persuading booksellers to stock books by authors who are completely unknown, the practice developed of supplying books to shops on 'sale or return'. In other words, if books do not sell, they may be returned by the bookseller to the publisher for a credit. But the publisher cannot return them to the printer: thus, unlike in any other form of retailing, the risk remains with the producer rather than the shop owner. This makes the finances of running a publishing company particularly difficult – you can never tell when the product is actually sold. The nightmare scenario for publishers is that the books have been subscribed into bookshops, the reviews are good, and you order a reprint just as the stock comes back from the shops for a credit.

Books are outstandingly good value for money

In industry, most firms would seek to make a profit of at least 15–20 per cent; publishing houses do well to get 5–10 per cent. As some wag once said, the only enterprise you take on for love not money is owning either a publishing house or a football team.

I think it behoves all authors to constantly restate the value that book purchase represents. A paperback novel costs less than a cinema ticket, or a large frozen chicken, yet there are still large sections of society that consider them expensive.

So, can you deliberately buy books (rather than anything else) as presents, give a talk in your local library or school to coincide with National Book Week, choose books to be photographed with, or just enthuse about them whenever possible? A head teacher I know consciously walks around school carrying a book in his hand in the hope that it will prompt conversations and encourage others to read. As we are producers of the codex, our aim should surely be to convert others to feel as passionately about books as we do. There *are* natural allies out there.

On the Chris Tarrant radio show[3], singer Rod Stewart was taking questions. This one came from Mike on the M1:

> Mike: Rod you are a rich man, you can have anything you want. What do you want for Christmas?
>
> Rod: I like books; particularly ones about trains. I love reading about trains and knowing things about them.

Similarly, the BBC's John Simpson was asked what single medium he could not live without:

> 'Books. Nothing – not radio, nor television, and not even the Internet – can replace the book for me. If books stop being published, I shall

3 October 2006

24

give up travelling, close the door and spend the rest of my life reading the ones that already exist. And I shan't switch on the television set, ever again.'

Summary of this chapter

Marketing may never have appealed to you as a subject, and you may have an innate hostility towards the very idea of your own writing being tinkered with or packaged to make it more appealing to fickle readers. Resist such thoughts.

1 If you engage with what marketing means and how your publishers are trying to market your work, you will be better able to assist them, and hence achieve the greater sales of your work that will cement your future relationship.

2 Authors rely on booksellers, retailers and wholesalers to find their most likely customers and sell to them. They thus have a moral responsibility to promote the industry they seek to profit from, and should do everything in their power to assert the power of the book in general, and the value it represents. Their relationship to the industry does not just depend solely on their ability to talk up their own books.

3

How marketing works in publishing

Marketing is much more important to publishers today than used to be the case. Until about 15 years ago, the industry was editorially dominated; most of the early decisions about the manuscript were taken on the basis of content, with discussion of how to make the product sell starting much later. Today, the vast majority of publishing houses are led by people from a marketing background. With books being sold through a much greater variety of locations (for example, supermarkets, garage forecourts, leisure centres and restaurants, as well as via the Internet), the marketing of books has had to become more professional. This is having a substantial impact on the kind of titles commissioned. Rather than remaining a product-driven industry – where products are created before the search for markets begins – the industry is now increasingly market-driven. Publishers try to identify market segments with specific needs, and then to produce the products to match.

Marketing in publishing: what happens and when?

Most publishing houses divide responsibility for different parts of the publishing process between different departments (editorial for content, marketing for spreading information and persuading people to buy, sales for achieving the orders, production for format, distribution for the mechanics of getting the books where they are needed). It is usual for senior staff from each of these departments (or perhaps just the appropriate director) to get together at regular intervals to discuss, and then hopefully approve, the plan to publish new titles. It is at these meetings that the idea for each potential new title will be discussed and the Marketing Director will present an outline plan for both the estimated size of the market, and how best to reach it; the Sales Director will be required to say how many they estimate are likely to be sold. Sometimes there is a single Marketing and Sales Director handling both plan and sales estimate; sometimes there are two individuals with separate teams. Whatever the case it is essential that they cooperate to establish the planned title's potential print run, and then see that plans are carried out and the sales estimate fulfilled.

Once a forthcoming title has been approved at this meeting, and money can be spent on it, the title's marketing and selling will be broken down into a series of stages that will be carried out by more junior members of the department.

Why don't books get larger marketing budgets?

It's important to address the realities of book marketing immediately. Unless you are a blockbusting author, or very famous for doing something else and your book is the by-product of another career, the marketing of your book will almost certainly not rely on the spending of large amounts of cash.

Why is this? Because books have low purchase prices and sell in relatively small quantities, so whereas a car manufacturer can safely allocate 2–5 per cent of anticipated turnover to the promotion of a new vehicle, the potential income is much greater than from a new novel that sells 15,000 copies in paperback (which, incidentally, is pretty good going). Be prepared: most of the marketing for books depends on regular and well-trusted mechanisms of informing the relevant stockists who will take the book, and strong pursuit of free publicity from the media who may cover it.

Rather than describing how marketing plans are formulated[1], I am going to concentrate on the points of contact between authors

1 If you want to know more about this, consult *How to Market Books*, by the same author, Kogan Page, 4th edition, 2008.

and publishers – the stages at which they may consult you, and what you need to do in return. Most of the following are routine procedures (those only relevant to books for which there are particularly high expectations are described as such).

Points of contact between author and publisher

An entry in the house database

All titles need basic descriptive copy for a range of purposes, from catalogue compilation and website to in-house newsletters and trade information, long before the accompanying manuscript has been delivered. This will be loaded onto the house computer system (or database) and recycled many times.

This first piece of descriptive copy about your book will probably be drafted by your sponsoring editor, based on the information you (or your agent) submitted to the house in a bid to be published. It should state the key selling points of both you and your book.

If you are asked to help

This is not the place for a complete biography; rather just two or three key attributes that qualify you to write the title in question are needed. The most important thing is to ensure that this copy remains up-to-date. Database copy is drafted very early in a book's life, and the content of the final book may change dramatically during the writing process. By final delivery, the title, publication date and even author name may have changed. So ensure that you keep the publisher informed about what you are doing, so they are promoting the title you are now writing.

The author's publicity form

At about the same time as your contract is sent out, you will usually be sent an author's publicity form (it may get overlooked, so do be sure to ask for one). There is advice on how to fill it out in chapter 9.

An advance notice (or advance information sheet/forthcoming title sheet)

The name of this document varies from house to house, but it is a constant throughout the industry.

An advance notice is routinely produced for each new book and will be sent to all who need to know about it (bookshops, reps and wholesalers, international offices, and so on). This is the first public information on the forthcoming title; it usually appears six to nine months pre-publication, and will be heavily used in persuading bookshops to support your book. The usual format is a single sheet, with the subject matter broken down under a series of headings (author, title, short piece of information on the title, publication details such as format and price). It will be available as both hard copy and an electronic document.

The basic differences between this document and the house database information are that this is for external, not internal use; it will also include a sales prediction. The advance notice should feature any information that gives an idea of how many copies are likely to be sold, thus encouraging the retailer to stock the book. This could include:

- The sales of the author's last title
- Any key trends in the media/in society that highlight the subject matter with relevant audience/population figures
- Publicity/promotion already arranged to support demand
- Brief details of the location of story or author which may help persuade local stockists to take more.

If you are asked to help

As the advance notice gets heavily used in the process of persuading booksellers to stock your title, ensure that your publisher has the most up-to-date information on you, your previous titles, and how they have sold (particularly important if you have changed publisher since your previous book). EPOS (or electronic point of sale – a till-point recording of what has been sold) will give them a strong idea, but any additional information you have should be passed on. For example:

> 'At a recent book signing in the USA, at the Romance Writers of America national conference, I sold 50 books, even though my titles hadn't been released or publicised in the USA, purely through contacts I had made through my blog. That's only a very small slice of the people who read the website, and I imagine the impact is much greater than I can see.'
>
> Julie Cohen, author

In particular, be sure to pass on any information if the book has now changed its title. If there has been any change since the contract was issued, it's important to pass on the information formally (by email or letter), rather than relying on a conversation/discussion. A title that changes its name between initial announcement to the trade and appearance of the book can cause endless confusion, and result in lower stocking.

A website entry
All houses now have a website, and details of your book should appear long before publication (unless they are deliberately withheld to secure a competitive advantage, and prevent another house from copying your idea).

If you are asked to help
(See also the information in chapter 11.) Begin by looking at their website as a whole; your contribution should mirror what is there and be mindful of the reader. If you find that every other author has one short paragraph about themselves, they are unlikely to award you ten.

The website is usually managed by a separate member of staff and updated at regular intervals. Make sure you find out who is responsible and keep them informed about any relevant details.

Try to provide *interesting* information – details that offer added value to what they already possess. Those surfing the net tend to have short attention spans, and reading a screen is tiring, so the copy should be brief and punchy. Most readers can spot a book blurb or jacket copy, and if they are searching the website for more information, regurgitating what they have already seen is dull. Quotations can work very well here, so if you have friends/contacts who could offer a relevant testimonial, be sure to provide it.

Is there a book in you?

A&C BLACK
Reference

Alison Baverstock

Alison Baverstock is a former publisher, author of 13 titles, publishing industry consultant, teacher of creative writing courses and advisor to new writers.

Location: Surrey

Publication Date:	June 2006	Price:	£8.99
ISBN:	978-07136-79328	Edition:	---
Previous ISBN:	---	BIC Code:	CGW
Format(mm):	198x126	Extent:	256pp
Binding:	Paperback		
Illustrations:	None		

Subject: Writing & editing guides
Readership: writers
Territory: -
Rights Sold: None

Many people feel they might have a book in them – but how do you know whether you have what it takes to be a writer, whether your writing is any good, what you should write about and whether you should dedicate proper time to begin your dream? **This book asks pertinent questions of you via a questionnaire** to help you discover whether there is a talented writer in you. Each chapter provides background to the relevant point in the questionnaire. Packed with **advice from experienced writers** including known authors; **P D James, Philip Pullman, Jacqueline Wilson, Margaret Drabble, Katie Fforde** and more. Expert advice from Daniel Roche (BA President), independent booksellers, publishers Helen Fraser (Penguin) and Ian Trewin (Chairman Cheltenham Literary Festival and administrator, Man Booker Prize), agents and creative writing tutors. **Foreword by columnist and writer Katharine Whitehorn.**

KEY SELLING POINTS:

* An **interactive approach** to solving that niggling question – each chapter offers a mini-quiz, with key questions to test your specific response to the main question raised.

* A grading at the end of the book helps you discover whether you should begin writing now, or stick to your day job!

* Extensive quotes from the experts: known authors, agents, publishers and booksellers

* Packed with examples from real writers – their books and their stories

* A **light but highly informed as well as encouraging guide** to help get you started: from an experienced author, former publisher, and advisor to budding writers.

Competition: No direct competition

Customer Services: Macmillan Distribution Ltd, Brunel Road, Houndmills, Basingstoke, RG21 6XS
tel: 01255 302692 fax: 01256 812558 email: trade@macmillan.co.uk
Editorial, publicity and rights: A & C Black (Publishers) Ltd, 38 Soho Square, London, W1D 3HB
tel: 020 7758 0200 fax: 020 7758 0222 email:enquiries@acblack.com

www.acblack.com

Remember that journalists often use websites to find out more about authors when they are writing from home late at night. Use this opportunity to spread information, to add pertinent detail about you and your books. Try not to repeat what is on your own website: your publisher may or may not allow a cross-reference to it (the decision may depend on whether or not you publish with anyone else).

A cover blurb

This is one of the most important pieces of marketing copy written. Surveys have consistently shown that whilst the cover design may encourage a potential purchaser to pick up the title, it is the cover blurb that persuades them to buy.

If you are asked to help
See the relevant information presented in chapter 5.

A catalogue entry

Almost all publishing houses produce catalogues at regular intervals: an annual catalogue with a listing of all titles; a complete catalogue of everything in print; and seasonal lists in between (usually spring/summer and autumn/winter) giving details of the highlights of that particular period.

Catalogues act as a shop window for the wares of a particular publisher. Entries in these publications may be short – perhaps just a paragraph or two, or maybe no blurb at all in the case of the complete catalogue – but they will still routinely reach the bookshops and key wholesalers in your market, and the many outlets stocking English language titles internationally. What's more important, they are kept and referred to long after receipt – especially by customer order departments and by shops which never get a visit from a representative.

If you are asked to help
Remember that catalogues are used for year-round reference, and get retained as reference material long after the selling period (in particular by libraries and bookshops that get few visits), so the copy needs to last and not be dependent on time-specific

information. They also present the company's wares alongside each other, so it is important that the words used to describe each title:

- Make its specific benefits clear
- Do not knock other titles (either directly or by implication – for example, saying that a particular diet book *is the only one the reader will ever need*, if the company publishes ten others, is not helpful. On the other hand, it's important that titles can be distinguished from each other, so a good idea to use different words from those used for other titles
- Is comprehensible to people who are not subject specialists but nevertheless have the power to circulate information to those they know might be interested (for example librarians, booksellers, reps, and those opening the post). It's always dangerous to assume that because the author and editor understand the copy, and the end user will too, no one else matters!
- Builds the publishing house's reputation for a particular type of book. The author can ride on the back of this; they may gain new readers out of the staple band who know a particular imprint and trust it.

Presentation at a sales conference

Many publishing houses use sales representatives to call (either physically or by phone) on retail outlets stocking books. Most houses brief their reps twice or three times a year at a sales conference, providing them with binders that list the forthcoming titles over that period, and any key facts that may help them to persuade retailers to stock them.

If you are asked to help

Very occasionally the author may be asked to talk to the reps – this is a really valuable opportunity. If you are asked to present, a 'performance' will be more memorable than a long description of what is in the book. Think carefully about what to wear and the impression you want to create, and try to provide a couple of anecdotes that they can use when calling on shops.

Presenters/brochures

Presenters are glossy, very high quality brochures that are used to draw a response from booksellers, wholesalers and key accounts. They are not produced for every title, just those for which the publishers have high expectations.

With very little time in which to impress a book's saleability on a buyer, an effective presenter can draw the appropriate 'wow' and the consequent stock order. Presenter information is likely to be very short on book content and author information, and will include greater detail on how the title will be promoted together with proof that this will work (based on the success of previous/similar titles).

Key account presentations

The purchasing power of the major retailers and the book wholesalers is enormous today, and special visits are arranged to brief them on the titles most likely to appeal. These are usually handled by the Sales (or Key Accounts) Manager, who takes along a marketing outline, cover artwork, author information and a copy of the presenter. It is not unusual for a cover design to be altered if an alternative version would produce a larger stock order.

Point-of-sale materials

This is the term (often abbreviated to POS, and called Point of Purchase or POP in other industries) for promotional materials displayed where high-profile books are paid for, such as boxes to hold large quantities of stock (usually called dump bins), bookmarks, balloons and posters. Their chief function is to persuade booksellers to take more stock (the dump bin is supplied free if full of books) and to remind the potential purchaser to buy, so the words used on them must be both interesting and legible (preferably from the other side of the store). The prominent panel at the top of a dump bin may not include the author's name or book title. This is sensible, as your book will appear many times, face-front, beneath.

Whilst POS materials are not routinely available – they are produced for titles for which the publishers have particularly strong expectations – there is scope for producing low-cost point-of-sale materials that still have an impact on the market's willingness to buy. As the producers of ink on paper, publishers have an ability to create such things much more cost-effectively than other manufacturers. The following can all be produced relatively cheaply:

- Postcards for handing out at the till
- Bookmarks that use the cover artwork
- Badges (particularly good for children's titles)
- Mugs
- Balloons
- Shelf wobblers (T-shaped pieces of card that sit beneath the books on the shelf and protrude to attract attention)
- Posters

Even if your publisher is not producing point of sale, they may still produce a 'showcard' for you if you are planning to talk. This is a poster-like piece of information announcing your book, presented on card with a stand behind it, like a photograph frame, so it will stay upright.

Leaflets and flyers (simple leaflets)

Leaflets and flyers produced for books are usually as multi-purpose as possible. The publisher will probably not be able to afford to produce a separate flyer for each occasion on which one is needed, but will try to produce stock that will meet most needs. For example, the same leaflet could be handed out at exhibitions, used as the basis of a mail shot (probably with the addition of an accompanying letter and a reply envelope), sent to interested enquirers, and given to authors for their own use. If you really want leaflets that detail a special offer for a particular occasion, it might be cheaper for them to sticker existing stock than produce a special reprint.

If you are asked to help

Provide quotations and testimonials that your publisher would not otherwise have access to (e.g. reviews in your local paper or that you have spotted on Amazon). If anyone says anything pertinent to you about your book, write it down and ask if they are happy for you to use it for promotional purposes – then feed it back to the publisher. New quotes allow them to freshen up their marketing materials.

If you are asked how much stock you would like, take plenty. It's much cheaper to increase the print run by 500 than to have to reprint later on (hence the answer, if you run out later and want more, may well be negative).

Direct marketing

Direct marketing means sending a sales message directly to the person most likely to make the buying decision, and cutting out the retailer in the middle. It's a very effective way to sell high-price and specialist titles. As titles of mass-market interest tend to have lower prices, it can be difficult to make direct marketing pay – although if you can reach people who love books, and persuade them to buy lots at the same time, then it can work well.

Direct marketing also includes telemarketing, 'off-the-page' advertising (advertising space with a coupon for the reader to fill in), website promotions and house-to-house calling … any method of getting the potential purchaser to say 'yes' directly to the producer.

Effective direct marketing copy is divided into smallish paragraphs, uses a simple vocabulary and is quite repetitive, because the market will seldom read anything from start to finish, preferring to 'dot around'. There is a real art to writing an effective direct mail piece, so before you protest that what you have been sent to look at does not reflect your book, do compare it with other direct mail shots.

If you are asked to help

Writing direct marketing materials is a very specific art, but mastery here will help you when writing many other promotional pieces. The basic principles are as follows:

- You must provide enough information to enable the customer to make a buying decision, so any questions that a customer could answer by looking at the product – were they in a bookshop – must be addressed. These include how the information was put together, the format, the quality of the binding, and so on

- Repeat yourself. No mailshot is read from start to finish; readers tend to dip in and out. It follows that the key selling points must be repeated so that they are not missed, although without using the same words each time

- Divide up the information so that it is easy to read. Space is what draws the eye in, not densely packed text.

Trade advertising

Advertising in the trade press forms an important part of most publishers' marketing. With so many new books being produced each year, it's a direct route to the attention of those making stocking decisions. Space may be taken in trade magazines to reach booksellers and persuade them to stock. In addition to the weekly magazines, there are regular publications of export or 'buyer' editions – huge additional volumes that list all the titles in the forthcoming season. As well as submitting editorial copy and author/cover photographs for their future titles, many publishers take up the option of advertising their books as well.

The logic behind an effective trade advertisement is to persuade the retailer to stock, so the copy will concentrate on anticipated demand for the title and the author's ability to deliver what the market wants, rather than specific details of the title in question.

In addition to advertising to reach the trade, publishers may put loose inserts in trade magazines or mail them directly, perhaps concentrating on those shops which specialise in the kind of book they are promoting. Most houses will have built up their own mailing lists of those who stock their books, but if not, the relevant trade associations can supply details.

Press advertising

Before publication, this is how most authors imagine that their books will be promoted – and hence often a major source of disappointment. The theory is that advertisements in the press reach readers and persuade them to buy. The fact is that there are now so many new media formats (for example, the vast range of magazines and broadcast programmes) that planning a 'media schedule' (or a list of where and when to advertise) to reach the entire market is both virtually impossible and hugely expensive.

But whilst more press advertising is the one promotional item that most authors say they want, many houses are now devoting attention to securing features through promotional arrangements (reader offers and 'sponsored editorial' in return for advertising). In any case, copy that appears as an editorial feature, even if sponsored (i.e. paid for), is more likely to be believed by the reader than advertising copy.

Space advertising in public places

Taking billboard space in the street is very expensive, so unless your book is likely to sell in huge quantities, it is unlikely to be affordable.

On the other hand there are cheaper options through space advertising in transport sites – on the sides of taxis, in the ceiling panels in the carriages of underground trains, in the panels inside buses, 'cross-track', on escalator panels and the poster sites on platforms and in passageways – because people are often squashed, can't get access to their own material, and are happy to daydream. And books make ideal products for this kind of advertising.

Promotions

'Promotions' is a loose term usually referring to the linking of two or more items for a joint push to a related market. For example, newspaper readers might be asked to collect tokens from consecutive issues of a paper towards a free book, or a promotion might be run offering subsidised books on the back of a cereal packet, in return for the customer collecting packet tops. Sometimes a special edition of a book may be produced as a giveaway or 'cover-mount' on a magazine. As books have a high perceived value and are seldom thrown away, they offer strong potential for use in promotions, but, given the cost and time required to set them up, promotions are relatively rare. They are more likely to be arranged for authors who have a strong appeal and a long backlist, or for a new imprint that a publisher is trying to establish.

If you have contacts of your own in this area, do pass them on – even better, get things started, and *then* pass them on.

Publicity and PR
Book-review columns offer a straightforward way to get coverage for a new book. But reviews are not your only option; many forms of media will be more interested in the author than the book, and feature space may be available for author publicity.

When you have written a book, a wide range of panellist/interviewee opportunities opens up: those who have written about a subject are assumed to be expert/interesting/both. Be aware that little details you would rather were forgotten, or which undermine your seriousness as a writer, may be hugely useful to those handling publicity. For example, what you have on your mantlepiece, the details of your first sexual experience, and how you feel about your childhood all form the basis for regular features in the press in which authors may appear. For further information, see chapter 10.

Merchandising
In a publishing context, this means selling further goods to the public which build on the success of the original book – for example, stationery, T-shirts, lunchboxes, soft toys and duvet covers, all of which refer to the original product. Some bookshops have the space to stock these items, but they appeal particularly to other retail outlets such as superstores, and serve to expand the 'shelf space' devoted to your book.

Other marketing activities
There are other routine marketing activities. For example, publishers attend international book fairs, and trade delegations may take relevant titles to exhibitions abroad. Many publishers advertise in the marketing materials put out by wholesalers and retailers, and others will take advertising space in relevant professional publications (for example, for the academic, educational or professional markets).

Summary of this chapter

An understanding of the established mechanisms through which your publisher will inform the eager world about your new book is helpful, as it will allow you to offer the right kind of assistance, and at the right time, in the marketing process.

Marketing budgets in publishing are low, because the unit selling price and the numbers sold in general do not yield a substantial sum to be ploughed back into marketing. It follows that any chance for speculative and cheap marketing may be followed up. You should not expect that all the activities outlined above will necessarily happen, or occur in the same order. It's also common for book promotions to be 'piggy backed' on each other so that costs can be shared over several contributing titles.

If you end up producing your own marketing materials (and many authors do), here is a checklist for you. Whatever the information you prepare, don't forget to include the following, in its most up-to-date form, so that ordering is easy:

- Author name (spelt correctly)
- If it is an edited work, i.e. lots of contributors, the editor's name (ditto)
- The book title (not its working title)
- The series title, if it is part of one
- Details of the publisher: name, address, website and contact information
- The book's ISBN (every book has a different International Standard Book Number)
- The price
- Which edition this is (if it has appeared before)
- Publication date (be realistic not optimistic).

With this information, any book can be ordered from any bookseller – usually at no extra charge (although a small deposit may be required). This tends not to be widely known, because most other industries don't work this way. In a supermarket you would have to order an 'outer' of 24 or 48 lots of your desired purchase. It's worth reminding customers just how easy it is to obtain books!

4

Preparing your manuscript for submission

When should you send your manuscript in to be looked at by an agent or publisher?

Writers want to get published, so at some stage they will need to start sending their work to agents and publishers in the hope of acceptance. But deciding that you need an agent or publisher at some stage is one thing; deciding that now is the time to start looking, is another.

It's important to start looking for an agent or publisher at the right stage in your writing career. Do so too early, and you risk compromising a relationship with those you might like to work with in the future. Show them work that is not ready, and they may conclude that you never will be:

'Don't send me your work until you are happy to be judged by it. There is no rush – get it right.'

Simon Trewin, literary agent, PFD

'In general writers have one chance to pitch a book to an agent or publisher, so it's important that you don't do so until you are happy with what you're sending them. It's the same with submitting to publishers as to an agent. I have one chance to get their attention with each new manuscript I offer. They may comment on what they don't like, but they will not want to keep seeing resubmissions of the same thing. Rather than taking heart from the new bits, they will spot what did not appeal to them in the first place.'

Heather Holden-Brown, literary agent, hhb agency Ltd

Are you fit for publication?

A friend I made when we were both expecting our first child had been a midwife. She told me she had prepared for having a family of her own by 'getting fit to have a baby'. She ran, swam and attended aerobics classes – all pre-conception. Her aim was to get her body in prime physical condition before the rigours of pregnancy and childbirth took their toll. It's an effective metaphor for writers. We need to develop some mental toughness and self-belief before we start seeking representation, so that we are in the best possible condition to nurture and present our writing to the waiting world.

> 'Rejection can be very difficult to take in the creative field. If you can retain that belief in your own work then you will be able to brush-off the turn-downs you receive.'
>
> Simon Trewin

What kind of response are you looking for?

What do you want agents and publishers to do for you? Are you looking for feedback on your writing; an indication that you are on the right lines? Or are you ready for that publishing contract right now? If it's feedback you want, you may be better off joining a writing circle, building one of your own, or relying on the judgement of those you trust.

Journalist and now writer Adam Powley, author of *We are Tottenham*, writes:

> 'If you are writing alone, having someone you know who can offer an honest and constructive opinion is key. The support of family, friends and colleagues was also a big help for me.'

Several writers say that it works best if those you show your work to first are not too close. Romance writer Jenny Haddon, who is published in more than 100 countries and 25 languages by Harlequin Mills & Boon under the pen name of Sophie West, comments:

> 'I have a loose association with two other writers. We all write very different books but we like each other's style and want to read each

other's work. We get together a couple of times a year to set practical goals and we then encourage each other. It works completely because we are different temperaments and don't compete with each other. It wouldn't work for everyone, though. We end up being pretty naked to each other. Not everyone is comfortable with that.'

Others formalise things a little more. For example, the Oxford Writers Group consists of 10–15 people who meet on alternate Tuesdays in each other's homes. They take it in turns to read about ten minutes' worth of their work in progress, and then they discuss it openly. But to give enough time to everyone wanting to read, they soon found they had to close to new members. They also had to abandon their email address because it received so much junk mail, and so have now set up a page on the secretary's own site: http://tinyurl.com/y9vd55. They recently published an anthology of their members' work. It's worth noting that such groups always attract more potential new members than there are spaces to fill, so you might think about starting your own. Here is some advice from someone who did just that:

'If you do start a group, the initial genesis may be clear – you and a few friends/friends of friends who have bumped into each other from time to time and had brief but meaningful conversations about the difficulty of writing. But if you decide to widen the group (and new blood is really healthy, particularly if the core group know each other very well), you should think very carefully about who else to include.

Some people join a writing group with the purpose (subconscious or not) of having their work applauded by an appreciative audience, and they are horrified if you start finding fault with it. There are others, perhaps a little further forward on the path to publication, who take this a stage further by assuming that the group is there to support them alone. You will spot them if you find that any conversation connected with publishing or writing soon becomes one in which their writing/character/success/ambition becomes the main instance. If you want to be honest with each other, then you need to be able to listen to constructive criticism, not expect unqualified praise – or attention. Some members can be too ready to demolish the work of others, without the vital "building up" first, and this can be equally difficult to deal with; criticism should always be given in the context of it being a greater thing to have bothered to write at all.

And then of course there are a load of sad souls – dare I say nutters – out there looking for something to join to brighten their lonely lives, who quite fancy the idea of writing a book. If your group is small, and it will need to be if everyone is going to have a chance to read, people need to feel very comfortable with the other members present. I would strongly advise you to ask people to send in a sample of their work and a letter telling you a little bit about themselves before you allow them to attend meetings. If you don't like the look of them you can say that their work is "not up to the standard of the rest of the group". You don't want the rest of your members to gradually stop coming, leaving you alone with the odd ball!'

The serious writer has to navigate a difficult path; they require sufficient self-belief to keep going, but an ability to listen to constructive and engaged feedback that may be useful to the development of their writing. And only you can decide where you are on this route. If you find you are so sensitive about accepting criticism that it threatens putting you off writing, you are not yet at the right stage to submit. Instead, wait until your ideas are more developed; until you are further on in both your writing and your ability to defend it without feeling crushed if someone else does not like it.

Other sources of feedback

Alternatively you could join a writing association and benefit from any manuscript review services they offer. The Romantic Novelists Association in the UK runs an excellent New Writers Scheme whereby other members review your work. Another option is to pay a manuscript review service for feedback, such as The Literacy Consultancy (www.literaryconsultancy.co.uk) who are opening a US office shortly.

Should you send off a partly finished manuscript?

If a house asks for three chapters and a synopsis, is that all you need to have completed? For a non-fiction proposal, this can be enough: they require an outline of your project and its market, a sample of your writing, and some information on you. For a fiction submission it's far better to have finished the whole book. If an editor or agent really likes what you have sent, finds it topical or can immediately think who it might appeal to, then that's a great start. If they then ring you to request more, and find out they already hold all that exists, there will be frustration – and your moment is lost.

For an illustrated children's book, getting to the right stage of readiness does not necessarily include assembling the pictures. Children's publishers deal with more illustrators than any author could possibly be aware of, and if they like the story enough, they will find the artist to match.

Agent Philippa Milne-Smith specialises in children's books:

> 'Whilst we don't need the pictures, an outline of what you see going where is really helpful; a mock-up showing how the pages relate to each other. The Ahlbergs (Janet and Allan, famous husband-and-wife author and illustrator team, and the creators of my all-time favourite baby book *Peepo!*) would send in tiny little versions of their new books, with all the writing in place. These were things of beauty that I longed to keep – but they showed how seriously they took the way their books should work.'

How to submit your writing

I hesitated over whether to include the following information; what follows may sound blindingly obvious to the reader. But after consultations with various publishers and agents, and hearing repeated instances of writers not thinking through when and what they send, guidance is perhaps needed – if only to reassure you that the detail does matter. If you don't care about what you send, why should they?

> 'When you take on only six new writers a year and get about 6,000 submissions, I know the odds don't sound good. But it is amazing how many writers slave away crafting a novel and then lessen their

chances by throwing together a shoddy submission package. You would never go to a job interview in old jeans and a t-shirt and the same applies here. Don't undersell yourself. If you follow a few rules you will find it much easier to be taken seriously by the agents you select. It's like learning a new language or riding a bicycle – once you master it, you will never look back.'

Simon Trewin

1 **Send a printed copy.** Even if you have built up an informal relationship with your publishing contact/agent, you need to be in control of what you send – and of how it will be received. Sending a file by email leaves it up to the recipient to print it out. If they do, they incur expense, which may irritate; if they don't bother to print it they may never read it – reading on screen is never as satisfactory. What if their printer runs out of paper or ink halfway through disgorging your file? Will they remember to go back and print out the rest? Will they print it out on paper that has been used on one side already, which means that the clarity and pleasingness of the whole will be reduced?

2 **Print what you send.** This sounds obvious, but hand-written submissions do occur. You may have read that famous writers like writing in beautiful notebooks, or on lined paper, but that does not mean that those starting out can do the same!

3 **Ensure that the typeface you use is legible, and the font big enough to read.** Use a conventional face, not the 'mock hand-writing' styles that are available. Some typefaces date quickly – think how tired **Comic Sans** or 𝕺𝖑𝖉 𝕰𝖓𝖌𝖑𝖎𝖘𝖍 now look – so choose something that is classic, and perhaps reflects the type of manuscript you are producing.

4 **Your manuscript should be error-free.** You would be surprised at how many submissions contain grammatical and spelling errors. Use a thesaurus and a book on grammar. Remember, you are writing for people who care about words and how they are put together. Publishers are not pedants, and they can spot a good writing idea even if the occasional error occurs – and of course a completely error-free manuscript does not guarantee

publication, as it may be dull – but poor presentation never helps. If you are breaking generally accepted grammatical rules, for literary effect, you must be consistent.

5 **Your manuscript should be clean.** A dog-eared copy contains a powerful subliminal message: this has been around the block a couple of times; other people don't want it – but might you? To send a clean copy you may not need to print out the whole thing again, the top few pages might do. Along similar lines, ensure what you send does not smell. Your favourite cologne, or the brand of cigarettes you consumed whilst working on the manuscript, may not be to everyone's taste.

6 **Print your submission single-sided, on clean paper.** I was handed a manuscript to look at during a writing conference recently, and it was printed out on pre-used paper. The minutes of a parent-teacher association meeting were printed on the back. The ink 'show through' was distracting, and the lack of care taken definitely reduced my concentration on what was in front of me. You want your *words* to engage the reader, not extraneous thoughts such as 'how on earth could they not have noticed that'.

7 **Most houses ask for manuscripts to be double-spaced.** Other houses want two or three chapters printed out in normal spacing, and will only require the double-spaced version if they want a closer look. Read their entry in the publishing yearbook and establish their requirements.

8 **Ensure that there is sufficient margin around the typed matter to make the page a pleasure to read.** Type that extends over the whole page is tiring to read (because it can't be 'absorbed' quickly). Think how the narrow margin in a newspaper column allows you to read down the middle and get the gist.

9 **Number the pages, and ensure that the numbers are sequential.** This can be tricky if you are printing out different chapters and each one is held as a separate file with its own internal numbering. If this is the case, you need to start the numbering for chapter two with the number after the last page of chapter one. Your word processor is able to cope – you have to use the button that says 'start the numbering from ___'. Think what

would happen if your manuscript got dropped on the floor: reassembling a series of chapters whose pages were all numbered 1 to 20 would be very difficult!

10 **Mark each page with your name and the title of what you are sending in.** Do this in small print, as a 'running head' or 'footer' to the page.

11 **Don't staple the pages.** The standard way of reading a manuscript submission is to turn the pages one at a time, from one pile to another (so don't send connected computer paper that the reader has to pull apart). A couple of rubber bands are sufficient to hold the whole thing together.

12 **Put what you send in a folder.** Instead of stapling, use a file or holder that will keep your pages together. This is part of your submission, so should be attractive and clean.

13 **Don't place tracking devices in your manuscript.** It's not uncommon for authors to place a 'checking mechanism' in what they submit, to ensure that the material has been fully read (for example, a hair or post-it note towards the back of the pages). Their assumption is that only if the submission has been read in full, can a decision be made. But think of the situation from the recipient's point of view. Why should the reader have to go through all your material to decide whether or not they want to publish it? Standing in a bookshop and trying to decide which should be the third of my 'three for two offer' I can tell within a couple of paragraphs whether or not I want to progress with a book, and it is these quick standards that the publisher will apply (because their reaction as a consumer matters hugely). They don't need to read every word to know whether or not they want to publish your work.

14 **Make sure you have removed from the package anything you did not mean to send.** Like the last rejection letter you received. It's so easily done.

15 **If they specify that return postage must be included, include it.** Attach it to a big enough envelope to hold what you have sent. And make it the right amount of postage – not part of it, hoping they will pay the rest (if they don't, the carrier will hold onto the parcel until you pay the difference, plus an

additional fee). Even if you think publishers make so much money from the authors they already represent that they can afford to pay the postage on what they send back to you, why should they? Remember: your manuscript is not the only one they will receive that day – on average they will receive at least 29 others.

16 **Put the whole package – letter, market description, synopsis and whatever they have asked for (see the next chapter) – in a clean envelope, preferably a padded one.** Don't use the extra-large staples to hold the parcel in place – most people hate undoing them. A bookseller of my acquaintance refuses to order from one house who sent out book orders like this; she had had her fingers ripped too often. Similarly, don't cover your parcel with brown sticky tape so that the recipient can find no way in. Make what you send a pleasure to deal with!

At what point should you chase a submission?

You want your material to be considered carefully, so don't rush the recipient. Even though you are desperate to hear from them, resist chasing too soon. It's a good idea to send a stamped addressed postcard so they can acknowledge safe receipt, but once you know your submission is there, give them at least a month before you follow up with a phone call or email (one or the other).

'Be patient. Today I had an author call me three times to see if I had read his work. It arrived yesterday! There is keen (which is great) and there is downright pushy! Leave it alone for four weeks – on many occasions you will hear back much faster, but sometimes there is too much going on to give you a speedy read.'

Simon Trewin

'I am quite robust with authors who demand a quick response. We did not ask you to send your material in, and if you want us to consider it properly, you must wait for us to do that.'

Victoria Barnsley, Chief Executive of Harper Collins, addressing the 2003 AGM of the Society of Authors

Summary of this chapter

1 Think carefully about why you want to send your material off to an agent or publisher. If you want confirmation that you can write, or feedback on how the story is developing, look for support elsewhere.

2 Build up your personal resilience before you start trying to get published. You will need it.

3 Get yourself and your manuscript into the very best possible shape before sending it anywhere. You can only make a first impression once.

4 Be careful how you chase. If you are too persistent, they may respond by just getting your manuscript out of their office as quickly as possible.

5

What to send with your manuscript

I will deal in the next chapter with the best recipient of your material (whether agent or publisher), but before we progress let's think about the overall package that you send.

What kind of response are you looking for? I am assuming that you want to get taken on as a client (by an agent) or as a published author (by a publishing house), or to maintain and improve your existing relationship with either or both (if you are already agented or published). As an author you almost certainly want attention, but if you want to be/remain published, you want the *right kind of attention*. And the decision on what kind of response to give you will be heavily influenced by how you manage your approach. Putting your manuscript in the post with a hastily written compliments slip and hoping for the best is never a good idea. You should give your manuscript the best possible chance of being positively received by appearing professional.

This chapter is divided into two parts. Firstly there is a short section on writing promotional copy – because that is what you are producing when you are writing to an agent or publisher to try to get them to take interest in you as a writer. Secondly there is discussion of the various pieces of information you need to draft to accompany your writing.

Writing promotional copy

Promotional copy consists of words that aim to sell. Writing it is not the same as writing an essay, or a memo to explain a proposition. You should always remember that the reader of promotional copy has a choice – to read or not to read – and consequently you must make it as easy as possible for them to absorb what you have to say. In achieving this, your most useful asset will be a grasp of the importance of selectivity.

For example, you may be able to think of 20 reasons why a potential reader should decide to represent you or publish your book, but you should probably restrict yourself to two or three; perhaps even just one, depending on the time and inclination of the market to listen to you. And do make sure that the one or two you choose are relevant to the market, rather than to your own interests (e.g. a whole new look at the subject offered in your new text for first year university students, rather than a systematic debunking of a much-quoted but erroneous theory of a rival).

Think first about the audience

Your starting point should always be to concentrate on the audience to whom you are writing. What kind of people are they; in what kind of circumstances are they reading your material? How much time do they have to read? What else did they receive in the same post? How interested are they in what you are describing? If you adopt this approach, your material is far more likely to be appropriate – and hence be read.

The needs and priorities of your audience must be uppermost in your mind all the time. Talk about what interests them and how your product meets their needs. Describe the advantages and benefits of your book, rather than its features. For example, instead of: 'This book includes a chapter on marital therapy,' consider: 'A valuable chapter on marital therapy allows you to try out the techniques that top consultants recommend.'

A good way of finding out whether your copy is sufficiently benefit-laden is to add the phrase 'which means that ...' to the end of every product feature you describe. For example: '200 top cooking tips included' would become '200 top cooking tips included, which means that you can start saving time in the kitchen immediately'.

Keep it simple

There is a temptation to dress up explanatory copy in long words, in an attempt to really convince. When writing promotional copy, however, it is usually far more effective to concentrate on simple benefits and promises, which can be grasped immediately. For example, instead of: 'A detailed explanation of marketing techniques that have been developed and practised over Mr Kenchington's entire career in manufacturing,' consider: 'Here is the wisdom gained from a lifetime's experience in industry.'

Along the same lines, try to write in the present tense, using words you are familiar with yourself (rather than ones that are part of your 'reading' vocabulary – words you understand but do not use in speech very often). A useful method of finding out whether or not your text is easy to read, is to read it out loud. If you stumble over particular words or phrases, or cannot reach the end of the sentence without needing to pause for breath, the odds are that it is difficult to read.

The words you use should be immediate in their impact, and are more likely to be of Saxon origin, rather than Latin. For example:

Saxon	Latin
news	information
now	immediately
hurt	injured
eaten	digested

In addition, try to use terms that are vivid rather than hackneyed, for example:

Vivid	Hackneyed
love	like
hate	dislike
adore	love
deranged	mad

Be very careful in the number of adjectives that you use. Try not to be 'over-regular'; for example, giving every noun two adjectives can get very boring:

- This useful and timely book ...
- This current and up-to-date title ...
- This accessible and readable manual ...

One, none, or perhaps three might be more effective.

Asking questions is a good way of involving the reader, provided they are not questions which attract a swift 'no' and a jettisoning of the promotional piece!

Link the sentences and paragraphs using easy-to-read phrases like:

- It follows that ...
- This means that ...
- In this way you can see how ...

Having said keep the text simple, the insertion of interesting and unusual words can be extremely effective if they are surrounded by simpler terms. For example:

> There was nothing to commend him but his smile. And she was surely too old, and had too much common sense, to be beguiled by a smile.

The use of 'commend' and 'beguiled' lend an intriguing aspect to this cover blurb for a historical novel.

For interesting words, use a thesaurus on a regular basis, and try to read good English and listen to articulate people – it's catching!

Match your vocabulary to the market

Promotional materials supporting a title should be written in a style that is appropriate to the book. Do not make a beach-read sound like a literary prize-winner, or a basic 'how to' book sound like a university textbook. People make very quick decisions on the basis of the copy you present.

They will also be very wary of buying from you a second time if they feel they have been misled the first. If they buy a book from you on the basis of copy and your product does not live up to the expectations generated, their disappointment will be remembered. This is particularly difficult if you are seeking to develop a brand image for yourself or the publishing house.

Be wary of jargon, or 'professional' speak. Many special interest groups, whether bound together through work or pleasure, develop an accompanying vocabulary. Such jargon serves to make those who belong feel a part of it, and those who do not, outsiders – and it is dangerous to use it in promotional copy. Why?

Firstly, because jargon changes all the time, so you can appear out-of-date very quickly – particularly if your promotional material will have a long life on someone else's shelves. Secondly, you are in danger of getting it wrong and making your promotional piece look out of touch or even ridiculous. Having said that, there may be certain 'buzz words' that you need to use to show to the market that this is a particular kind of title (e.g. 'textbook', 'reference title', 'saga', 'bedtime story').

Pay particular attention to issues which may offend your market, and make no assumptions about it. Never assume that all fire fighters are male or all nurses female; you will annoy them, and everyone else will be aware of the gaffe.

Aim for a tone that is reasonable and hard to disagree with, rather than one of academic argument refuting any suggestion that a title is not needed. Clichés and puns can be useful for making a sales proposition seem familiar, but I tend to avoid outright humour.

Effective design makes copy easy to read – and act upon

As you write, think about how the text will appear as a pattern on the page. The key thing to look out for – and avoid – is predict-ability. Always remember that writing promotional copy is very different from writing essays; formulaic writing suitable for work that has to be read in order to be assessed will not do here. An introduction, three or four dense paragraphs of copy, all of roughly the same length and number of sentences, followed by a conclusion, will most likely fail to engage the reader's attention. Essays have to be read in order to be marked; readers of promotional copy have a choice. Dense copy is offputting, so break it up using bullet points, short paragraphs and subheadings. Try to vary the length of sentences and paragraphs so that the overall effect is enticing.

Keep the measure of the text (the width over which the text is spread, from left to right) on the narrow side, so that it can be read easily. Wide text measures tire the eye, and tired eyes stop reading. The same goes for other design techniques, which serve well in small quantities to attract attention, but can be very wearing if over-used. For example:

- Using too many CAPITAL LETTERS
- Reversing large amounts of solid text out of a colour (out of a photograph is even worse)
- Justifying text so that the blocks of copy appear solid
- Fitting text around photographs and illustrations so you end up with a ragged left-hand margin
- Making the typeface very small or very large
- Using too many typefaces
- Using clashing colours – for example, bright blue on a bright red background.

All of the above can work well when used in small quantities to attract attention, but have the opposite effect when over-used. They make the words difficult to read.

What information to draft to accompany your writing sample

If you are planning to approach agents or publishers with a view to being/carry on being published, you will need the following. Some authors send them all together; others send a letter first (perhaps by email) followed by the others if requested.

A&C Black Publishers Ltd
38 Soho Square
London W1D 3HB
Tel: 020 7758 0200
Fax: 020 7758 0222/0333
Email:
enquiries@acblack.com
www.acblack.com

12 July 2006

Dear Course Leader

We understand that this is the time of year when university lecturers update or confirm their reading lists for the academic year ahead, and are therefore writing to tell you about a new book that we hope will be relevant to all students taking, or thinking about taking, courses in Creative Writing.

Is there a book in you? is a serious examination of the resources needed by those who want to get published. It looks at the likely consequences, financial, personal as well as emotional, of a determined ambition to write. It makes ideal reading for anyone considering a course in Creative Writing, and we hope it will be a **valuable addition to the reading lists for both potential and enrolled students.**

> "I am very impressed. It's not so much an instruction manual as a huge consultation panel drawn from a whole range of different experts and I can't imagine any writer, aspirant or established, not finding it absorbing and enlightening. The Questionnaire gives it a real punch, and I thought the section on 'Is There Not a Book in You?' particularly heartening and intelligent." Professor John Carey

The author, Alison Baverstock, is a former publisher as well as author, and now teaches Marketing and Creative Writing at Kingston University. Her other books on publishing and communications have been very well received, *How to Market Books*, now in its 4th version, is a set book on university courses teaching Publishing Studies, *Marketing your book, an author's guide* – is also very popular. To see Alison talking about the book visit www.meettheauthor.co.uk and follow the links to *Is there a book in you?*

Is there a book in you? is based on an extensive period of research with writers, of all levels of success, from the very famous (Philip Pullman, Jacqueline Wilson, Margaret Drabble), through the 'mid-list', to those who are seeking to get published for the first time. Her feedback is realistic and pragmatic, addressing the 'how you will feel' as much as the 'how to'.

> "I wish I had had this book when I first tried to get published."
> Katie Fforde, novelist

> "Admirably practical and realistic advice on what it takes to become a writer. I was impressed." Mark le Fanu, General Secretary, Society of Authors

This new title joins our extensive list of books for writers, including the well known **_Writing Handbook Series_** and of course the bestselling **_Writers' & Artists' Yearbook 2007_** which is celebrating it's **100th edition** this month. Details of all our writing books are enclosed, and can also be found on our website, www.acblack.com. For information about the huge *Writers' & Artists' Yearbook* creative writing competition running in conjunction with The Literary Consultancy from 24th July visit the new dedicated minisite, www.writersandartists.co.uk.

Yours sincerely

Vicky

Vicky Atkins
A&C Black

Chairman Nigel Newton *Managing Director* Jill Coleman
Directors Janet Murphy • Oscar Heini • Colin Adams (finance) • Kathy Rooney • David Wightman • Jonathan Glasspool
Registered Office 38 Soho Square London W1D 3HB England • Regd no 189153 • VAT no GB 215 0391 03
Distribution Macmillan Distribution Ltd *telephone* 01256 302692 *email* mdl@macmillan.co.uk

Copy for a direct mail letter. Note how the reader's attention is drawn to key points of the text through design effects such as indenting, bold and underlining.

- An introductory letter
- A synopsis
- A CV
- An outline of the market
- A book blurb

1 An introductory letter (called a 'query letter' in the US)

An effective letter introducing your book is vital. Every package should go with an accompanying letter, not just a hastily written compliments slip or a post-it note. It may be obvious from the size of the parcel that what is enclosed is a manuscript, but forget the letter and you lose a really big opportunity to impress the market; a bit like failing to introduce yourself when you meet someone for the first time.

Some recipients will read the manuscript you send, and some the synopsis, but *all* will read the accompanying letter. Writing an effective one may take you a long time, but it is well worth the trouble. It should outline all the basic information: what kind of book you want to publish, how far down the road you have got, what is noteworthy about you as a person, who else thinks so. Start with the interesting bits, not the predictable ('I enclose an ms and a stamped addressed envelope' is quite a boring beginning to a letter that you are hoping will ignite their interest in you as a writer), but be careful to avoid gimmicky, jokey, angry or arrogant approaches.

The whole thing should:

- Be well written – you are writing to people who care about words

- Be not too long (don't waste their time; you want to direct them to the manuscript enclosed rather than tell them everything about you). One side of the page is plenty

- Look attractive (it is the spaces on a page that draw the eye in, not the text, so paragraphs of different lengths and a ragged right-hand margin really help to attract the reader and keep them going)

- Be printed on decent quality paper, in an easy-to-read typeface (nothing gimmicky) and signed with an ink pen rather than a blotchy ball-point
- Be knowledgeable about the agency or publisher being approached (nothing is more likely to win friends). If you have emailed to find out whom to send your material to, ensure that you spell their name correctly
- Begin well (according to David Ogilvy, the copywriting guru, the first 11 words are crucial)
- Describe the project briefly (in no more than two or three sentences) so that the reader is clear about what kind of book is on offer, and wants to know more
- Never say at the end of the letter that you'll telephone in a few days to follow up your submission – it sounds rather menacing (but do phone or email to check on progress if you haven't heard anything in a month or so).

Some agents and publishers acknowledge what they receive; others do not. You could ask them to email receipt, or enclose a stamped addressed postcard with a reminder to let you know they have received your submission. This is a further opportunity to remind them you are a human, so try a witty postcard or add a caption to an image to make the point that you are dying to hear from them! For inspiration, look at the card selection in a local art gallery and think which picture sums up your mood as you wait for them to respond. But do bear in mind that some small agencies or publishers only deal with the unsolicited submission pile every few weeks, and so may not return what you send immediately.

Here is the advice of an agent on writing an introductory letter:

'Life is short and less is more. No letter should be more than one side of A4 and in a good-sized (12pt) clear typeface.

Sell yourself. The covering letter is one of the most important pages you will ever write. I will be honest here and say I find selling myself very difficult, so I can see how tricky this is – there is a thin line between appearing interesting/switched-on/professional and arrogant/unreasonable.

The letters that include phrases like "I am a genius and the world doesn't understand me" or "My Mum thinks this book is the best thing she has ever read" (of course she does – that is her job!) don't exactly fill my heart with longing! In your pitch letter you are trying to achieve some simple things: you want me to feel that you take your work seriously. Wear your writing history with pride. Tell me about that short story you had published or that writing course you attended and the fact that you are writing alongside a demanding job or in the evenings and weekends when the kids are asleep. Tell me why you write – I love hearing about the different paths that have led people to the moment when they think "I want to write".

Tell me who your influences are and tell me about the book you are sending me. A few lines will do the job here; I just want to get a sense of the territory I am going to enter. Tell me what you want to write next. Hopefully you won't be following your commercial romantic comedy with a three-volume science fantasy epic or vice-versa! At the end of your letter I want to feel in good company and ready to turn the page. I am not interested in seeing what you look like or how old you are – we are not running a model agency here! Publishing isn't as obsessed with age and beauty as you might think, but it *is* obsessed with finding distinctive new voices. And a final point: get a friend to read the letter and give you some honest feedback. Put it to one side for a day or two and come back to it – distance is a great editor.'

Simon Trewin, agent

Case Study

The Night Attila Died: Solving the Murder of Attila the Hun
by Dr Michael Babcock

The following letter was sent by an academic teaching at a US university and resulted in responses from three agents willing to take him on. The book was published in July 2005.

Dear [Literary Agent]:

I am seeking representation for a non-fiction book entitled *The Night Attila Died: Solving an Ancient Murder Mystery*. I am a college professor with a PhD in medieval languages and literature from the University of Minnesota and a MFA in Creative Writing from the University of North Carolina. [1]

Historians tell us that Attila the Hun died on his wedding night in 453 AD. Drunk and flat on his back, he died of natural causes – an internal haemorrhage. The only problem with this account (and it's a big one) is that it's a complete fabrication. *The Night Attila Died* challenges 1,500 years of history by presenting evidence that Attila was murdered and that the truth was covered up in the official imperial records. [2]

The events and characters are among the most interesting that history has ever assembled on one stage. There's Aetius, the ruthless Roman general and boyhood friend of Attila who defeated the Hun in a decisive battle in Gaul. There's the weak and stupid emperor, Valentinian III, who pulled a dagger from his robe and assassinated Aetius in a jealous rage. There's the emperor's older sister, Honoria, who secretly plotted to wrest power from her brother and managed to start a world war in the process. [3]

In the eastern Empire, the characters are just as colourful: Emperor Theodosius II, a weak ruler who bungled the first assassination plot against Attila, and Emperor Marcian, whom I accuse of masterminding the plot that finally destroyed the Empire's greatest enemy. Throw in, for good measure, a scheming eunuch and a pathetic little dwarf named Zerko. It's a great set of characters. [4]

But what the book is *really* about is philology. The textual science pioneered two centuries ago by the Brothers Grimm is the tool that lets us peel away layers of conspiracy and propaganda. Through the philological method we can reconstruct what really happened and how the conspiracy to kill Attila was covered up as official history. Chapter by chapter the reader participates in the detective work. In the end the threads of an ancient conspiracy are revealed and the verdict of history is overturned. [5]

There's more at stake than just a good detective story. This is ultimately about what happens when two cultures with irreconcilable worldviews collide. It's how we confront the Other with all the power of the sword and pen. What emerges from these violent confrontations is a skewed understanding of the past. We may call it history, but it's often just propaganda. *The Night Attila Died* is rooted in the historical moment of the late Roman Empire, but the conclusions I draw are deeply connected to our own time. [6]

My publications to date are academic, in particular a book on the literary representations of Attila. I am uniquely qualified to write *The Night Attila Died*, having spent 15 years studying the historical and literary records as preserved in Latin, Greek, Old Church Slavonic, Old Icelandic, Old French, and Middle High German. (But that isn't keeping me from writing a lively narrative!) I am recognised as an expert in this field and have consulted for a History Channel documentary on "famous deaths". As an enthusiastic and dynamic speaker who speaks widely at conferences, I intend to promote the book aggressively. [7]

May I send you a full proposal with a sample chapter? [8]

Sincerely,

Michael A Babcock, PhD

Commentary (keyed to the paragraph numbers)

[1] Direct introduction. No beating around the bush.
No 'clever' attempt to hook the agent.
Identify the type of book it is.
Briefly identify yourself and your credentials.

[2] The hook. What's unique about this book?
Why should the agent keep reading the query letter?

[3] What you're trying to demonstrate in the body of the letter is your style, your personality, and the 'interest factor' of the subject itself.

[4] With carefully selected details, you can pique the interest of the agent. Agents and editors love books – that's why

they do what they do. So show them what the pay-off will be for reading this book. You are also conveying the depth of the subject and your expert handle on the material.

[5] Establish the significance of the topic and its relevance. Establish points of contact with general knowledge (the Brothers Grimm).

[6] Again, this draws out the significance and timeliness of the subject – that is, you're trying to answer the 'So what?' question.

[7] Return to your credentials and qualifications to seal the deal.

[8] End with a direct, unambiguous appeal that requests a specific follow-up action.

How it worked

'This letter was sent out by e-mail (I decided to focus only on those agents who accepted e-mail enquiries). Of the ten, I heard back from nine and all nine wanted to see the full proposal. Of these nine I had three agents who were interested in representing the project and one, in particular, who pursued it aggressively. This agent called me up and expressed such enthusiasm for the concept and my writing style, that I felt he was the natural choice. Even though there were better known agents who were interested in the project, I opted for the lesser known agent on the theory that he was highly motivated to sell my book. The book sold in less than a month. There were three editors who were interested in making an offer on the book; in the end it came down to two and the higher bid won out. As a side note, the book sold on the strength of the formal proposal and a single sample chapter.

The book was sold in December 2003 and submitted in final form to my editor in July 2004. It was published in July 2005 by Berkley Books.'

2 A synopsis

Most publishing houses and agents specify that a synopsis should accompany any manuscript submission. What exactly a synopsis consists of is much less clear. Here is some guidance on how to prepare one.

For fiction

This should be an outline of what kind of book you are writing; it is *not* your chance to give a detailed listing of what is in each chapter. The synopsis should start by ensuring that the recipient can grasp immediately and precisely what kind of book/writer is on offer. Specify what kind of writing genre it sits within (e.g. saga, literary, science fiction, romance, etc.).

> 'The synopsis should be no more than one side of A4 and should tell me the narrative arc of the whole book so that I know what happens after the first 10,000 words. Simple as that.'
>
> Simon Trewin

In her excellent book about selling commercial fiction, *From Pitch to Publication*, agent Carole Blake says that the synopsis should answer the following key questions:

- Whose story is it? (Make it clear who the central character is.)
- What do they want and what stops them getting it? (What is the central character trying to achieve, and what are they up against as they try?)
- How do they get it? (Is the plot compelling and page-turning?)

Describe the action, and lay out the plot in the order the reader will encounter it, without doing it chapter number by chapter number. Describe the characters in brief and compelling detail, without a full 'back story'. Give a word count if the book is finished; estimated extent if not.

For non-fiction

Publishers are trying to fill gaps in non-fiction publishing, so it's essential that what you send shows how your book fits with existing material – what fresh information do you have; what new insight can you bring?

If you can, quote which section of the bookshop your title would be stocked in (don't just say the table at the front!) and list subjects/well-known examples of books already existing in this category. Booksellers are loathe to stock titles if they don't know where to put them, and agents may be unwilling to back a title that has no natural home. A friend of a friend wanted to write a book on the menopause and to call it *How Long Before I Can Hang-glide?* A bookseller persuaded her that whilst this would make a very good subtitle, people looking for books on the subject would be in danger of not finding it – unless they were by chance looking in the sports section too.

- Say what the competition is, and why your book is different
- Sum up the market for the book, with facts, figures and snippets of interesting information (did you realise that rats make better pets for children than hamsters and can recognise their own names?)
- State your credentials for writing the book. Be imaginative; things you take for granted may be interesting to others
- Non-fiction is often accepted when still in draft form, so say how far you have progressed to date, and when you will have a manuscript ready by
- Does it need illustration?
- Give a word count.

The importance of the title

Whether you are writing fiction or non-fiction, it's tempting to think that writing the book is the really important thing, and that the book title can grow out of the writing later. Wrong. The title is hugely important: it should catch the agent's attention and stick in the memory. Think how the same thing works for you with films and plays: a good title can pull people in. Literary novelist Joanna Briscoe received a whole new level of attention when her third book was entitled *Sleep With Me* and given an enticing cover. (Previous titles, *Skin* and *Mothers And Other Lovers*, although well reviewed, had not sold as well.)

'The title matters hugely. I want something that excites me, something that will draw a similarly instant reaction from any publisher I mention it to. So go for something that is topical, intriguing or witty and to the point.'

Heather Holden-Brown,
hhb agency Ltd

3 An accompanying CV

You may already have a CV on file. If so, it's probably left over from when you last had a proper job, so begins with your formal education and progresses through the jobs you did, in order, concluding with your interests.

'A classic summer page-turner ... it is hard to get this book out of your head'
OBSERVER

Sleep With Me
JOANNA BRISCOE

Start again. As an author trying to engage interest, you need to tempt them with fascinating and relevant details. Neither agent nor publisher is the least bit interested in how you did in your school exams. What they *do* need to know is what makes you a compelling proposition as an author. Remember that everyone is interested in how 'promoteable' any potential new author is.

'*Marketable* is a very debateable term; I know many authors dislike it, and of course the quality of the writing is the most important thing. But I have to think of a way of talking about the client to a publisher that will engage their interest.'

Clare Alexander, agent

This could be your job, your family commitments or your past experience. Don't assume that what you consider boring or mundane will be viewed in the same light by those you are approaching.

A background working in the City is not the normal path to becoming a novelist and so may be well received by an agent. Similarly your domestic arrangements may be ordinary to you, but interesting when combined with the fact that you have written a book. Take an imaginative approach to your past and think creatively. A friend of mine once used a revolving door in an American hotel at the same time as a well-known actor and would proudly boast that she had 'been around in New York with Cary Grant'. I have four children and have always moved house mid-pregnancy, hence the scan and the birth never took place in the same hospital. Whereas this is entirely a function of my husband's peripatetic job, my publishers got quite excited when I told them. What have you done that can be made to sound interesting? (For more advice on how to get noticed, see chapter 10.)

Your own marketability as an author is also very important to the decision-making process. A publisher may be unduly swayed by whether they think you will obtain publicity at the time of publication, so if you sound interesting here it can be a great help.

Trawl through your CV, thinking about what you have done in the past that is relevant – this could be something you have written, or taken part in. For example:

- Have you spent any time in a retail environment? This will have taught you that people can be very fickle!

- Have you had letters published somewhere relevant?

- Have you had to research or write reports (perhaps as part of your job) for a wide circulation? This shows you can get to the bottom of a tricky situation and explain it clearly

- Have you spent time in a playgroup? This, and/or being a mother, will have taught you how to manage your time, and that trying to keep the attention of small children is difficult

- Have you had any experience of PR? This will have revealed how important it is to identify and then get through to certain taste barons who have huge influence

- Have you given any interviews on local radio? This is very good practice for promoting a book.

Professional CV writers specialise in turning quite ordinary work or life experiences into significant-sounding events, so try to do the same.

In particular, be sure to indicate:

- Your previous published writing, if you have any
- Any awards you have received, or acknowledgements of your literary judgement (e.g. being asked to judge a prize)
- Any information relevant to your writing, for example if you have visited the country you are writing about or have a personal insight into your subject (e.g. you are writing about post-natal depression, having suffered from it yourself)
- Your commitment to your writing – be sure to mention it if you have already started on your next novel.

4 An outline of the market

When an agent approaches a publisher to enthuse about a new author, they will have to justify the claims they make on your behalf. The newer the feel of what you want to write, the harder they will have to work: it's not good enough to say 'everyone will want to read' this new title. So, find out the viewing figures for programmes that relate to the book you want to write, or the sales of magazines that have a strong overlap with your material.

Think laterally. For example, I co-wrote a book about parenting teenagers, and at the time I was trying to pitch it, there was very little published in this market. Most of the publishers I was talking to were in their early 30s and desperate to get pregnant; they could not imagine the teenage years to come. Looking wider, it seemed to me that our subject was really modern morality; how to provide guidance in a fast-changing world when people are terrified of being insufficiently 'PC' and saying things are just plain wrong. To prove there was a market I took as examples the book sales of popular philosophy titles by AC Grayling and the number of people who have taken an Alpha Course (2 million in the UK so far), and I also looked up the number of teenagers in the UK. The agent I approached told me this widening of the issue really made a difference to how he viewed my proposal, and it was published as *Whatever! A down to earth guide to parenting teenagers* by Piatkus in 2005.

So, on a single side of A4 paper that accompanies your publishing idea, outline its market potential. Try to answer the following questions:

- What is it? Romantic novel or business manual, travel guide or 'how to' self-help book?

- What are your qualifications to write it? Try to keep these brief, relevant and interesting, using emotive language (for example, 'author detests dogs' rather than 'author is afraid of dogs')

- What will this book do better than any other source of information/enjoyment available? Can you quantify these benefits? For example, 'buying a copy of this manual will save the purchaser thousands of pounds in accountancy fees'

- What kind of people will buy it? Can you define them clearly (job title, social standing, what they watch or read, etc.)?

- How much disposable income (or budget, if it's a professional title) do they have?

- How many are there of them and how contactable are they? The latter is crucial – a targetable society or mailing list is the genesis of many a published product. It doesn't matter if the resulting market is small in size; the important thing is that their desire or need for the product, and ability to purchase, are real

- What trends in society does your book highlight – for example, news events, popular concerns, audience viewing figures/magazine circulation of relevant publications? Has anyone notable said anything in support of this recently? If there's been a pithy article in the press about the same subject, attach a photocopy as proof, with the key sections underlined or highlighted.

Proof of the market or of your value as a writer
Endorsements are enormously useful. It is assumed that you will consider your book worth reading; far more persuasive is the opinion of an objective outsider. This could be in the form of an extract from a review – but of course a first edition will not have

access to reviews until after publication. So, if you are a first-time author, or your book is a departure from your usual kind of work, think carefully about who you could get to endorse what you have written. Go through your address book and think about the past – who could give you a useful plug? If your book has particular relevance to a subject that is currently very topical, is there someone whose opinion would be influential if it appeared on the book jacket? The person providing the quote does not have to be a celebrity (although if you know one, that's always useful), but what about other readers, writers and friends with relevant job titles?

Asking for endorsements is not as difficult as you might think. Some people will like to be asked (it's flattering); some will oblige out of pure friendship; others for the publicity it may bring them. Scan the local paper to find out if there are any locally based famous people who might endorse your work. On occasion you may even be asked to draft the kind of thing you would like them to say. This may be because they are short of time, or because they want to ensure that they write something appropriate. Whatever the reason, it's a wonderful chance to write your own review for their approval.

If you have no endorsements or quotes, consider whether there are any official publications that you can quote. These may have nothing to do with your specific publication, but if they prove the need for the product, or give the storyline validity, they may be considered relevant. For example, a novel based on medical incompetence could benefit from being promoted in conjunction with news coverage of hospital staff shortages or recent medical disciplinary cases.

Wherever possible, break down the statistic into the personal. For example, instead of:

'Last year there were 850,000 cases of medical negligence'

how about:

'10 per cent of hospital admissions result in a case of medical negligence' or:

'If you are admitted to hospital, you have a one in ten chance of something going wrong'.

If you are writing for children, ask a parent to read your stories aloud and give you a pithy comment. Or ask children to provide you with a quotation on why they liked it. If you have had your novel read by friends, ask them what they thought of it. You may think you have written a searing indictment of the modern world; they may just read it as an up-to-date thriller.

5 A book blurb

Think about what goes on the back of most books and how important it is in attracting attention to the title inside. A book blurb should be a fair representation of the style of the book; it should tempt the reader to want to know more – now – and should not give away the ending. Writing a book blurb is harder than you think, and is an excellent way of getting yourself noticed.

How to write a book blurb

Stand back and hover above; try to create mood, feeling and value for what you have written, rather than describing it in endless detail.

Case Study

The perfect blurb

I was about halfway through the writing of my book when I was asked to write a blurb for the back cover. The opportunity struck me as a highly significant one – here was my chance to sum up the value of the book, in a permanent format. This was all the more welcome because the book had been agreed upon so quickly. It had grown out of a chance meeting with the publisher, and as I am part of the market, and know exactly who I am writing for, it had taken me less than two days to draft a contents list and knock out an introduction and first chapter. And on this basis the book had been commissioned.

Since then I had been busy researching and writing the title, and uncovered a real need for the book I was writing. I felt passionately that the advice I was about to give would be well received, and very strongly that the group I was writing for were underrepresented and badly served by existing information sources.

I viewed the chance to write the book blurb as an opportunity to elevate the professionalism of the group I was writing for. I drafted a full page of closely argued text which I felt proud to have written and which other writers were complimentary about. We all felt better about ourselves as a result. Two days later I realised that what I had written was a manifesto for a possible professional association of author-marketers, not a book blurb, and of course I would have to start again.

What a good book blurb should contain

A book blurb is there to entice a purchase, not to justify a lifelong career or calling. Bear in mind that such blurbs are often read in crowded places particularly beloved of pickpockets, with shoppers jostling round you whilst your other purchases dangle from your other hand, and that books are often heavy and thus difficult to hold for a long time. It follows that there isn't time to take in lengthy copy.

A non-fiction book blurb should give a quick indication of whom it is for and why they need it. A fiction blurb should both convey atmosphere and indicate what kind of book it is (mass-market or literary fiction). Quotes are extremely valuable to both fiction and non-fiction as they can pinpoint accurately what kind of expectations the reader should have.

I also think it's very important to match the words to the product. Do not make a romantic novel sound like an entry for a literary prize: you will put off both potential markets.

Here is the opening of the first paragraph of one of my favourite fiction book blurbs, for *Behind the Scenes at the Museum* by Kate Atkinson. The specific details and unexpected combinations (I love 'conceived grudgingly') are intriguing, and the copy made me buy the book:

Ruby Lennox was conceived grudgingly by Bunty and born while her father, George, was in the Dog and Hare in Doncaster telling a woman in an emerald dress and a D-cup that he wasn't married. Bunty had never wanted to marry George, but he was all that was left.

Summary of this chapter

Most writers assume the only thing that really matters to a would-be agent or publisher is their writing. Whilst this obviously is (or should be) the basis of an agent or publisher's primary interest in you, you can substantially enhance the impression you make when you introduce your material, and thus make it more likely that it will be read and responded positively to.

Only once you have thought about the issues covered in this chapter are you ready to approach agents and publishers.

6

How to find an agent

At workshops on how to get published, the question of whether or not you need a literary agent often comes up. Does every writer really require one?

Quite simply, having a literary agent (or an agent of any sort, these days) helps you get published. If an agent has taken you on as a publishable proposition, publishing houses are far more likely to take notice of you too. If you are writing non-fiction, or for a highly specific market (e.g. Christian; gay; professional), your need for an agent may be less urgent, as careful research into which firms publish the kind of book you want to write may guide you to the right home. For writers of fiction, having an agent helps hugely – although it is said today that it is more difficult to find an agent than a publisher.

Literary agents perform a very valuable sifting function for publishing houses. They are people with lots of publishing experience, who are offered many potential books in various stages of development. Those which they favour, they will bring to the attention of potentially like-minded publishers. Of course that's not to say that all great potential writers have agents, or that all new authors taken on by publishing houses are similarly endowed; just that amongst the newly published, there will be more authors with agents than authors without. Stories of what go on to become best-selling books being spotted on a 'slush pile' (the pile of unsolicited manuscripts that all publishing houses accumulate) *do* occur, but they are memorable precisely because they are rare. Most successful writers have agents.

How do you attract the attention of a literary agent?

Many agents have been publishers themselves. It follows that they like to specialise (usually in the kind of books they used to publish, or those in which they have a strong personal interest) and that they have an encyclopaedic view of the industry. You can find a list of agents in industry yearbooks, along with a list of the best-known writers they represent. JK Rowling found her agent through this source, and apparently initially picked him because she liked his name (Christopher Little).

Agents often work a bit like advertising agencies, in that they tend to have just one major client in each field. So just as an advertising agency would not represent two directly competing accounts, a literary agent is unlikely to take on two authors whose books are very similar. This is particularly true in the non-fiction market, where having two directly competing authors would be bound to cause difficulties.

Generalising further, literary agents are gregarious, fond of being noticed (they tend to dress quite strikingly), good talkers (they certainly seem to know everyone), dramatic travellers (fond of hopping on and off planes in a blaze of self-generated publicity), good negotiators (their livelihood depends on it, as does that of the authors they represent), and not immune to vanity – so mentioning that you have heard them speak, or making it clear that you know who they are and particularly want to be represented by *them*, tends to go down well. Most are based in key hub cities, although there are clusters in other attractive places, close to publishers. It's not necessarily more prestigious to have a metropolitan agent:

> 'I find we are often seen as a bit fresher than the London agents, and all publishers seem interested in finding out about the literary scene in Scotland.'
>
> Jenny Brown, whose agency is based in Edinburgh,
> but who nevertheless sells most of her clients' work
> to London-based publishers

Before asking what they can do for you, consider what's in it for them

I always think the secret of a good business proposal is to look at it from your would-be collaborator's viewpoint rather than your own. Thus, when seeking sponsorship, you get a far better response if you explain what the potential sponsor will get out of a relationship with you than if you tell them how much you need the money. To paraphrase JF Kennedy, 'Think not what an agent can do for you, but what you can do for an agent.'

Taking the same approach with agents, they are looking for writers:

* With talent (and can you prove it by providing quotes from satisfied readers/reviewers?)
* Who can sustain it beyond one book (and thus will be ongoing earners and repay the initial investment of time they make in you)
* Who are topical (all agents and publishers claim to be looking for the 'next big thing')
* Who are different, or have a new slant to bring to an existing strand of publishing
* Who are *promoteable* (a key publishing term meaning interesting or memorable to the media). How you come over (or are likely to come over) in the press/on the air will be a key factor in deciding whether or not to take you on.

How the money works between author and agent

The money side of things needs a little more consideration. Whilst most agents are book lovers, and enjoy what they do, their service does not exist as a wider service to literature in general, but to make a profit. As well as a talent for writing, they are looking for financial remuneration from those they represent. So whilst an agent may be willing to help you shape your novel and provide advice, they will be doing these things in the hope that you will reward them with books that sell, rather than out of pure altruism.

It's not uncommon for authors to feel that agents have picked them up, sounded interested in them, asked them to reshape their writing (and often at short notice), not managed to get them published – and then callously dropped them. They are left feeling deflated and bewildered about what to do next. But looking at the situation from the other side of the fence, if no money has changed hands, or no long-term agreement been signed, the agent may feel that the investment in time and money has been largely their own – and for no ultimate financial remuneration.

Whatever advance[1] the author gets, their agent usually gets 12.5–15 per cent of it, so it is in the agent's interests to sell the book for the highest amount of money – or to the publishing house that is most likely to make a long-term success of the writer's career. This may lead the cynical to conclude that agents are more likely to be interested in media-friendly (or just media-based) authors than pure literary genius, but it is through the success of key names that they are able to take a punt on new writers. An agency that confined itself to literary fiction alone, and ignored the popular market completely, would probably not last long.

Top tips for finding an agent

In the attempt to help you find an agent, here are some top tips for securing their attention.

Do your research
Consult the list of agents in industry yearbooks; look carefully at the kind of writers each agent represents, and note their specialities.

---

1 Money up front for writing a book, usually repaid out of 'royalties', which is the amount earned by the author every time a copy of their book is sold. Royalties are usually based on the share of receipts, and so vary according to the discount at which stock has been bought – so if a supermarket receives a high discount, it will mean the author gets a lower payment. Once the advance has been 'earned out' (i.e. sufficient copies have been sold to pay off the advance received), the author starts to accrue royalties direct, and they are usually paid twice a year.

If they say they do not take science fiction, do not assume that you are helpfully extending their range by offering it. Send an email outlining what you have in mind and ask who is the right person within their firm to send it to. Don't assume that if the agency is called 'Snodgrass and Wilkins' you must talk only to one of the two key names (who may in any case be long dead): the chances are that their books are full already. A more junior member of staff may be hungrier for new authors, and don't forget that their judgement will be backed – because they are a staff member and presumably have been taken on by the partners to widen the range of those they represent. And one day they too may be on the letterhead. All agents assume a far greater awareness of their own firm than a well-educated individual may have through simple general knowledge, and are fond of referring to it swiftly, and in abbreviated form.

'Do your research. Even though I clearly state my preferences on www.pfd.co.uk I still get letters saying things like, "Dear Simon – I know you don't like science fiction but I thought you might make an exception in my case," or "Dear Mr Terwin [sic] – I am sending you my whole 180,000-word manuscript instead of a sample as I want you to read the whole book now." This isn't helpful! Check *Writers' & Artists' Yearbook* for which agents represent your kind of writing and seek them out. Find out who represents authors you admire and approach them: www.google.com should give you the information you need, and BookTrust's information line also has a fantastic database.

Check contact details and make sure your letter is sent to the correct address. Spell names right – I am plagued by Terwins, Trewits, Truins and Treewins or even sometimes Strewin! These may seem like small points but they are all about presenting yourself professionally.'

Simon Trewin, agent

Send in what they ask for, not more or less

Submit your material in exactly the format they ask for: three chapters and a synopsis means just that; it is not code for 'anything over three chapters' or 'as near as you can get to three chapters'. And 'three chapters' means three sequential ones, preferably the first three, not just any old three. What you send should be accompanied by the elements outlined in the previous chapter.

Sole submission?

Some agents want to be sure that what you are submitting has been sent to them alone – and that you will wait until they respond before you offer your work elsewhere. If you are doing this, make it clear (add the phrase 'this is a sole submission' to your accompanying letter). Others take a more market-focused view, and will understand that submitting sequentially to one agent after another may take ages. But all of them expect straight-forward dealings from those whom they might represent:

> 'Be honest. If you are sending your work to more than one agency at a time, then let me know that in the letter. If I was looking for an agent I would most certainly write to more than one person at a time. All I ask is that you let me know this is what you doing. It is soul-destroying to spend a weekend reading a full manuscript that I have called in only to discover on Monday morning that I have missed the boat because another agent signed the author up on the Sunday. If it is a race, then let me know!'
>
> Simon Trewin

Keep going in your search

Remember that agents are individuals, and perhaps more indivi-dualistic than the key protagonists in many other professions. Just as many are instantly recognisable, so they also have very individual tastes. It follows that what does not appeal to one, may well appeal to another.

> 'There are as many opinions out there as there are agents prepared to read your work – keep going until you make a connection.'
>
> Simon Trewin

So if your first choice does not immediately sign you up, there may be others who think you are the next best thing since sliced bread! But they will only find out about you if you have the gumption to keep going. In the long run, getting an agent on your side is invariably worth the effort.

'We receive at least 20 unsolicited manuscripts a day; our books are full, and to be honest we are looking for reasons to say no – but I still get such excitement from a really new voice writing something that grabs my attention. I have known the world stand still as I ignore the rest of the post and just read on until I have finished. When that happens it's really special – and I will fight to get that author published. Sometimes it takes years, but if I believe in an author I will keep going.'

Carole Blake, Blake Friedmann

Case Study

'"So, how do you feel about publicity?" asked my brand-new literary agent, the one who'd told me excitedly that she "couldn't put my manuscript down". It was this enthusiasm, along with comments along the lines of "I see you as the next Mary Wesley" that made me think, not "There! I KNEW I was terrific!" but, well, perhaps, after all, I'd written something that others might want to read. But what do I know? I'm published, but not as a novelist, and I don't live in "the literary world", although I do know something about how it works.

Guided by her, I spent six months editing my ms – but willingly, because if you write for the love of it, rather than to bestow your precious pearls on the world, you're quite happy to be guided.

This is where things came unstuck. Although she kept saying she loved the way I wrote, she didn't like my opening chapter, seemed diffident about the alternative I sent in, then questioned the direction of my plot. I lost confidence, and began to struggle. Although I emailed her to reassure her that I was "pressing on", a four-month period of silence was followed by an email, out of the blue and copied to four strangers, saying that she was moving on, that she'd enjoyed working with me, and good luck in the future.

Whilst I'm in no position to comment on my agent's judgement (either of my own ability or of the market for middle-class, middle-brow fiction where there's no helpful "celebrity" angle), I accept that, quite simply, my first novel just wasn't good enough. But I admit I was disconcerted by my agent's seemingly instant acceptance of its failure, in view of the fact that I had been the restraining one in terms of enthusiasm. There is no doubt that she was always friendly, and I know she feels she did a lot for me.

Call me slow, but I was never exactly sure in which direction she was attempting to steer me. She was very clear that she knew "the book market", but when it comes to subject matter, it is a fact that she is younger than me, and (was then) single and childless: I felt confident that I'd lived in the real world, both professionally and emotionally, and had a lot of experience of the particular market towards which she was aiming me: women's book clubs.

In terms of our working relationship, of course I'm aware that she had people more valuable than me (by that I mean bringing in money!) to look after, as well as other new writers. I myself have a pretty busy life, so I hope it doesn't sound too pathetic to say I assumed our first meeting might be over lunch, or something similar! But we met twice in her office, and each time she made it clear she was going out, so didn't have too long, which made it hard to relax with her. I was never introduced to anyone else at the agency, and no contract was ever discussed. I think it's fair to say that the rejection of my novel placed a question mark over her judgement as well as my ability; so I needed her reassurance that she really did know how I should present my writing to a publisher – but I was too wet to ask.

Maybe this story exposes my naivete as well as a distaste for confrontation, but I honestly don't think I expected too much from my agent. I know about dealing with both failure and success, but this experience has left me confused. The writer's job is to get on with the writing; and I used to write at a gallop, neck stretched, nostrils flaired, but now I flounder. I've lost my momentum.

But I still write every day – and, for now, my challenge is to simply re-learn how to write for pleasure – which I suspect, ironically, might make me more marketable.'

Author

Choose wisely

If you are lucky enough to get attention from several agents, and are required to make a choice, the time-honoured way of getting to know each other sufficiently well to take the relationship further is for them to take you out for a drink, or even a meal. At this stage the power rests with you, but remember that if you do sign up, the agent you select will be taking a percentage of everything you earn. Who will push your interests harder? Whom do you get the best vibes from? Sharing income you have created with someone you really don't get along with may be fine if you feel that they are securing you better deals than would have been possible otherwise, but if you come to feel you are being given insufficient attention, it may just be irritating.

'Choosing an agent is a bit like getting married, and you need to be equally cautious. Love at first sight seldom works – so don't leap into an arrangement with the first one who offers to have you. Before you sign, talk to publishers about how they respond to the one you have in mind. Treat their answers with a degree of caution but keep your antennae bristling – are they putting you off someone who will strike a better deal than you currently get (good for you), or because they personally can't stand the sight of them (not so good for you). Think clearly about what you will do for each other; look each other in the eye. Meet and talk, for goodness sake. Consider a pre-nup. But once you are married, stick with it, and work at the relationship – for the sake of the children, in the hope that they might grow up to be best-sellers.'

Stewart Ross, addressing the AGM of the
Society of Authors, September 2006

'I spent last week selling myself to an exciting new author. So far we have had three meetings and as many conversations – not to mention countless email exchanges. The author is now auditioning three agents and I have my fingers crossed that she comes my way. If one agent wants you, the chances are you are going to be in a happy position of being able to choose. Appointing the right agent is the most important decision you will make – they can make and break careers.'
Simon Trewin

Leave your agent only after careful consideration

Continuing the marriage analogy, falling out of love with an agent is of course perfectly possible. Think carefully, though, before you take any drastic action.

If the problem is one of your writing confidence, or panic about a deadline, your agent may not be the best person to contact first:

> 'Do not have a crisis meeting with your agent. When it comes to the terror, agents are with the enemy. The last thing they need to know is that their client is cracking up.'
>
> Terence Blacker, author

Instead, try to talk through your options with an objective friend or colleague. Discussing the options out loud, and with someone who is not emotionally involved, often makes the problems seem more manageable or helps you realise that perhaps they should be communicated in a different way.

If you do decide on drastic action, and that moving on is your only option, leaving an agent is in theory a simple process. You serve notice, according to the terms of your contract, and try to find someone else. Timing can however be tricky. You cannot leave an agent who has already started touting your new book (so if you have discussed it with them to the extent that they are able to say they have been selling it for you, you will have to wait until your next book).

But as I have repeatedly said, getting – or remaining – published means you are operating within a buyer's market. There is always someone younger, prettier, and cheaper than you available to write, and you may not find it as easy as you think to find another agent. Agents and authors do fall out, and there may be fault on both sides, however wronged either party feels. But the simple truth is that both other agents and publishers will be wary of authors who have hopped from firm to firm, concluding (perhaps not entirely unfairly) that such authors find long-term relationships difficult, and will be tricky to deal with. And there is always another author available ...

The other difficulty about leaving an agent is that you leave behind, with them, the books you worked on together. In the future they may not be best motivated to secure good deals for that work. Be careful.

Summary of this chapter

1   It is easier to get published if you are represented by an agent than if you are trying to do so on your own.

2   It is harder to find an agent than a publisher.

3   Agents are experienced but opinionated; it may take you a while to find the right person.

4   Keep going in your search, but all the while maintain a sense of objectivity. Could it be that the collective negative opinion from those you have approached should tell you something about this particular project and its likelihood of eventual publication?

7

Approaching a publisher directly

You may decide to try to find an agent; alternatively you may decide to go straight to a publishing house. This chapter is designed to show you how (although you should also read the previous chapter, as many of the same considerations will apply).

Your starting point should be to buy a copy of a trade yearbook[1]. These have been the catalyst of many writing careers, and buying a copy is part of taking yourself seriously as an author. Here you will find a complete list of all the major publishing houses. Your second port of call should be the website of your local association of independent publishers: in the UK, the Independent Publishers Guild represents 480 firms (www.ipg.uk.com), and in the US, PMA – the Independent Book Publishers Association – has 4,000 members (info@pma-online.org). On their sites you will find many more options, largely specialist publishers broken down into the kinds of books they produce. Finding out just how many exist can be daunting. Who on earth do you approach first?

What kind of book is it?

Visit a bookshop and decide where your book might sit. In what section, and in what fellowship? Then look to see who publishes in this area. Note down the names of the firms involved in order to contact them.

Thinking about who else writes your kind of book is a very useful way of categorising your writing. As so many new titles come out each year (over 130,000 in the UK; 210,000 in the US),

1 *Writers' and Artists' Yearbook* in the UK

publishers often try to sell a new name on the back of an established one, so new writers may find the line 'In the tradition of Catherine Cookson' or 'The new John Grisham' on the front cover of their book. Such comparisons do not have to be book-related, and may have more street credibility if they do not. Can you describe your book in terms of a film or television programme? Penguin described Eoin Colfer's *Artemis Fowl* as '*Die Hard* with Fairies'.

Do the thinking for your potential publisher. Without being ridiculous (avoid comparisons with Shakespeare, and don't make an easy-to-read thriller sound like Salman Rushdie), with whom could your writing logically be compared? Get a second opinion on what you have written in order to better describe it (see chapter 4, for more on this).

The right kind of publishing house

Most publishing houses specialise. There are very few that publish poetry, and not all publish fiction. Being specialist allows them to work on the kind of books they like (it's their money they are spending, and however much you might wish they would publish in your area of writing, it is up to them). It also enables them to penetrate the market more successfully – they will have built up good links with reviewers and the book trade in their area of specialisation, and the latter will consequently take seriously any titles under their imprint. So offering them a title when they publish no others in that area would be a hard act to pull off, because they have no in-house expertise in that field. (Don't assume that you are helpfully extending their range for them; they may not want it extended.) Directories of publishing houses list their specialisations, and how they like material to be submitted. Many will not accept unsolicited manuscripts, while some insist on you sending return postage. Remember that the manuscript is sent at your own risk – never send your only copy.

Do you have any useful connections?

If your next-door neighbour is Editorial Director of Random House, then arguably you have a head start (although you might decide it is too embarrassing to ask them for help!). But consider carefully whether you know someone who works within the industry, and if you could approach them.

The department they work in really does not matter; if they work in the post room you could still ask if they could lay your precious words in front of the right person to make a decision. Bear in mind that whereas this would be immensely helpful to you, they might also be quite pleased to do it. As a very junior member of staff in my first publishing house I would have been flattered to be asked to be part of this process – and very proud if what I had 'found' turned out to be publishable. But remember that if you are asking a favour, you must be prepared for the person approached to give a negative answer – without either of you feeling awkward about it!

Before you get in touch

The person who will ultimately make a decision about your manuscript is the Commissioning Editor, so look in your yearbook, find out the name, and contact them by email to check that the current incumbent is the same person you have listed.

Some publishing houses specify the name of a general department to which material should be sent, such as 'Submissions'. If you are writing something that generally fits their list, you may be happy with that instruction. If on the other hand you have a specific imprint in mind, it may be worth sending an email to the firm to briefly outline your idea (one or two sentences is enough) and asking for the name of the most appropriate person to send it to.

If you are given a name, do ensure that you spell it correctly. Most people notice mistakes in their own name immediately.

The 'slush pile'

Most publishing houses receive a huge number of unsolicited manuscripts every day. Collectively they are often known as the 'slush pile'. There are stories of manuscripts being taken from the slush pile and turned into best-sellers, but it has to be said that these are told because they are so unusual. The more you can do to help yourself get to the top of the pile, the better.

How to attract the attention of those reading the slush pile

Most publishing houses pay readers to go through these manuscripts and deliver a judgement on whether or not they are saleable. Thus, your manuscript may never be read by a member of staff from the house you have approached. The judgement of the readers is not infallible (the Harry Potter series was rejected by many of them) and is also under siege because they tend to read so many bad submissions. It follows that those authors who, as well as asking to be published, also indicate who might buy their books, are at an immediate advantage (so follow the guidance in chapter 5 on how to prepare for this).

Joining your profession – societies of authors and other support organisations

Once you have had a book accepted for publication and have a contract from a commercial publisher (not from a vanity or self-publishing firm), you are eligible to join a society of authors (www.societyofauthors.org in the UK), and this is a very wise move. As well as holding regular meetings they also offer a contract-checking service – a detailed examination of the legal terms of publication – which is immensely useful. An agent can do this too, but the Society's advice is free. Attend their events and parties; listen to the speakers. Writing can be a lonely business, and it's reassuring to meet others in a similar situation.

You may also decide to join a relevant organisation for your type of book (e.g. for crime or romantic fiction, or for academic authors) and to start reading the publishing industry press.

Summary of this chapter

1 If you have a clear idea of what kind of publishing house might be interested in your writing idea, it's a good plan to make a specific and targeted approach to them.

2 They will need to be convinced by all the same things as an agent: your writing talent, longevity and marketability.

3 Think carefully whether or not you have any exploitable links within the book business, however unpromising.

8

Managing without a publisher: when to go it alone

Making the decision

There are various reasons why you may decide to self-publish, rather than seeking the services of a professional firm. For example:

1 You want the book published more than you want a commercial success. For example, if you are writing in order to preserve your family history or to set the record straight about something you consider important, you may decide that having printed copies is more important than gaining a commercial publishing deal.

2 You are completely convinced by your book idea, and want to be taken seriously by a commercial publisher. It is true that some books do get picked up by publishers on the basis of the author's commitment, both financial and emotional, to producing the first edition. The logic runs that if the author is prepared to commit their own funds to getting into print, it may be a worthwhile investment to follow.

3 You are very specific about how you want your book to look, and so plan to produce a limited edition at your own expense to show how the product might best be produced. (Incidentally, this is how Bloomsbury came across Ben Schott's *Original Miscellany*. He had produced 50 copies of his book of lists, at

his own expense, and it was seeing one of these that persuaded the publishers to take him on.[1])

4   You know more about the market than any publisher could. For example, if you want to write a book about your professional area of expertise, and have both a greater market knowledge of the subject and a more complete list of potential customers, it is arguably unreasonable to have to share the profits of the enterprise with a publisher who is not able to contribute in equal measure. And whilst you may know little about publishing, you can always buy-in expertise to cover areas you don't know about; writing magazines offer the names of several firms offering this kind of service.

5   You are fed up with publishers saying no and feel you have a good idea. You decide to go ahead anyway, learning what you need to know along the way:

'I was wasting too much time waiting for publishers. I am an artist. I have to start.'

Chantal Zakari, US self-published author of *Web Affairs*

Of course, it may be best for a commercial publisher to take on your book – because a third party is investing in you, and few would-be authors know much about production, distribution or marketing. But if you do decide to go it alone, you will need to think about the following.

Is there a market for your product?

If you decide to publish yourself, you must be doubly sure of the answer to any question a commercial publisher would want to ask. And two of the first would be: how large is the market, and

---

1   The story is that the book was created in this format, privately funded at first, and then found its publisher. In fact, Schott is clear that he had no intention of ever publishing the book when he was writing and designing it; rather, it was for his friends – and because he so enjoyed typesetting. He was however persuaded by a friend to send a copy to Nigel Newton at Bloomsbury, and was amazed when they wanted to publish: 'Only in retrospect did it seem like a clever move to create the book first, to formalise the look and the design of it. And it's to Bloomsbury's enormous credit that they let an unknown miscellanist loose with the design, content, jacket, etc. of a new book.'

what proof is there that it exists? If no book on your subject already exists, it may be that you have no competition – but equally it may be that there is no market. If you are planning to publish the title yourself, you will be assuming the risk too, so your maths must be correct!

Are you confident you can sell it?

Being passionate about your subject is not enough to persuade everyone with an interest to part with money for your book; and getting the information to the market can be very hard if you have not done it before.

It helps if you enjoy the selling process. Even if you do not, you must not feel demeaned by offering the product for sale yourself. I was interested to hear recently that part of the training process for new recruits to the insurance industry is to sell a product to a member of their own family or a friend, to overcome any initial squeamishness over the sales process. Terence Frisby, playwright and author of *Outrageous Fortune*, his self-published autobiography, commented:

'The author should never be embarrassed about asking for money for their book. I was quite resolute about this – after all, my friends know that the only time you get free seats in the theatre is when the show is no good. I was confident that the price was value for money for a good read in a high-quality hardback binding.

My second line of argument in defence of the £16.95 price (£18 with postage) was that I had invested £10,000 of my own money in the project and so could not afford to give it away. I always offered potential customers the chance to have their book(s) signed for no additional cost, or even the chance to buy one of the rare unsigned copies!

My real disappointment was the retail book trade. I felt they were utterly apathetic when it came to selling my book. Time after time friends would report to me that they had tried to obtain my book in bookshops but had been informed by booksellers either that they had never heard of it, or that it would take six weeks to order from the publisher, when in fact it was on the database and could be obtained in 48 hours from the distributors, a well-known, reputable firm. This appalling attitude merely spurred me on to greater efforts. I sold lots as a result of after-lunch speaking engagements, book fairs and theatrical groups.

Out of a total print run of 2,000 I have sold over 1,500. I did not recover my costs (I never thought I would) but the project has brought me huge personal satisfaction.'

For guidance of what kind of marketing materials you will need, see chapter 3; how many of these you are able to produce will depend on your budget. You will also have to allow for a certain number to be sent out free to booksellers and reviewers in the hope of encouraging an order or a review/feature.

What format?

Of course there are printers who can lay out and print a manu-script for you, but effective publishing involves far more than that. The retail market today is obsessed by format. The impact of design and lifestyle programmes on television and features in the media has made us all much more style-conscious than was the case even five years ago. Attractiveness of format now plays an increasing role in our decisions as consumers.

Commercial publishers have experience in choosing an appro-priate format for each product under consideration. Sometimes, relatively minor product adaptations may make something acces-sible to a much wider market: for example, adding more illus-trations or a more appealing cover may vastly increase a title's saleability. For professional books, aimed at a specific market, format considerations may be less important, and it may be effec-tive just to match the format to an existing style. In the case of a book being bought for its illustrations, the main product considerations would be the quality of the photographs and the comprehensiveness of the volume's content. The size of the book is less important and could just be made to match other photographic compendia on the market.

If you feel that the style of the book you want to produce is a crucial part of its overall appeal, you may either decide to run with the professionals or employ the services of a book designer.

Making the text easy to read: the role of the editor

Book editors face the difficulty that if well done, their job is absolutely invisible; the author's meaning shines through and the reader is never exposed to the stylistic problems that got in the way in the original manuscript.

The standard of editing in books published today is a subject raised relatively often in the media: there are frequent complaints of sloppy presentation and poor grammar making it through to the final product, and industry commentators say increasingly that publishers see editing as a cost rather than a necessity. And if the author's need for the publication is greater than the market's insistence on absolutely perfect text (for example, academic titles, where to be published is essential to the professional reward system), authors regularly report that they are offered financial inducements to ensure that the editing costs as little as possible. They may even be offered a financial incentive to deliver a 'pre-edited' text, which means it will receive no further editorial attention in-house (but of course that does not mean none is required).

If you decide to publish yourself, it is almost certainly worth ensuring that what you say is easy to read, and you may consider employing the services of a professional editor. You can find one by contacting a professional organisation for freelance editors and proofreaders. Jane Tatam of Amolibros (www.amolibros.com), an agency specialising in self-publishing, commented as follows:

'I have always had strong views about self-publishing. I've been in the publishing industry for nearly 30 years, and set up Amolibros about ten years ago with a view to helping authors self-publish, and providing professional assistance throughout that process. It seemed that the marketplace offered a choice of "do-it-yourself – but not very well" or being ripped off by a vanity publisher or so-called "self-publishing firm", who would also give poor professional support for even more money.

I know the industry well and hate the often snobbish attitude that both publishers and agents can have towards self-publishing. The self-publishing industry has been so beset by crooks – often called vanity publishers – who feed on people's hopes and then disappoint them, that the result has been to blame those seeking self-publication rather than those who seek to defraud them. That is an enormous pity, because self-publishing has enormous potential. It represents the ultimate freedom of the press, and given the way many of the large publishing companies are now run, is a valid alternative for the presentation of new and exciting talent.

Even established authors turn to self-publishing from time to time. It is not a crime, nor a method of publishing to be derogatory about. (Called private publishing in the 19th century, it was once the respected pastime of the peerage.) It should be celebrated in much the same way as the Edinburgh Festival Fringe, as a showplace for emerging and interesting talent, and I believe eventually it could have a real place of merit. If bad manuscripts are self-published, ultimately that doesn't matter – the industry proper is just as guilty of doing that. But every now and then there may be a real gem, and for that it is really worth it. There is also enormous potential with informative and professional non-fiction writing, where knowledge of the marketplace can give the author a head start over the conventional publisher. Finally, as a method of archiving personal information, which may not be valued now, except within a limited marketplace, but could well be highly significant in years to come, not least for research purposes, it is invaluable.

Nobody should ever delude an author into believing it is easy to make a profitable success out of self-publishing – it certainly is not, particularly in the areas of fiction, poetry and memoirs; but it can be an enormously satisfying process. The sooner writers start thinking about marketing, the better. It is best to realise from the outset that the majority of bookshops are unlikely to be supportive and are often prejudiced against self-publishing. Other ways must be sought, starting with pre-publication quotes from supportive worthies, and going on to designing direct mail campaigns, giving talks and offering to write articles. Even fiction can be sold this way, if the storyline has a solid 'peg' on which to hang the marketing. The Internet is fast becoming a good way to sell books but its contribution should not be over-estimated!

But every book that is self-published needs some loving care and professional attention to detail with regard to both the finished product and the marketing of it. That is exactly what I try to provide at Amolibros. There is no handy formula for this – I get to know my authors, help them reach their objectives and provide a personal service coupled with professional expertise and a thorough knowledge of the industry and how it works.'

Approaching the market

Sending out the book for feature or review

One of the most useful assets to anyone trying to achieve publicity for a new book is a string of contacts who can review or feature it in the media. Authors are fortunate in that most newspapers and broadcast media have feature slots devoted to covering books – no other industry can rely on guaranteed space/coverage. What is more, the potential of both author and book can tickle the fancy of features editors as well as stimulate a story on the news pages – there are lots of opportunities for coverage. You may even become the subject of an in-house battle over space: different section editors like theirs to be the most popular.

The link between coverage in the media and boosted demand for the book is clearly established. Having said that, bear in mind that there are also lots of different publishers competing for this space, with so many new titles coming out every year. A publishing house will probably have access to one of the databases that keeps track of who is the relevant correspondent for each publication/programme. This is a very workable system and, with luck, a press release sent to the right person will result in coverage. If you are doing it yourself, you will need to be resourceful about finding out names and resolute in following them up. Here is some basic advice on putting together a list of contacts.

1 Never assume interest from anyone, even if it's someone you have known since you were four years old. All contacts have to be worked at. Internal politics can ruin your chances – someone higher up the ladder may hate you; they may be jealous or consider you an upstart; lots of authors review books and you may have commented negatively on their cousin's

book and have thus generated ever-lasting dislike – writers can have very long memories. Even if your book is topical and newsworthy, external forces can drive you off the page; war may break out; a key figure die (think of the luckless authors launching new books in the week after Princess Diana died).

2 Think about who might review your book. The first names on your list will be easy (those you read yourself), but a great way to start building up a media contacts list is by reading and watching other media, in particular those you wouldn't usually see. Media reading is a habit. We tend to read the papers we agree with, and as they confirm our prejudices, we can maintain a cosy idea that the world thinks as we do.

Tabloid newspapers are easier to read (and often better written) than the quality papers (what used to be called the broadsheets), yet if you compare the readership figures you will see that the papers' circulations are hugely different, with many more reading the tabloids. Ironically, tabloid readers account for a greater proportion of book buyers than readers of any other newspaper (because the circulation figure is so much higher, the percentage of regular book-buyers is correspondingly larger).[2]

Look out for the names of relevant correspondents and in particular for 'reader offers' – the kind where the journal provides editorial coverage of a product and readers can write in for a free sample/copy. Most magazines will be happy to arrange such a deal, because it boosts reader loyalty, and the author benefits from endorsement because an editorial mention is far more influential than advertising copy (and also far cheaper).

3 Don't forget the local media. Even if you never read the local press, don't assume everyone else feels the same. Local radio stations and papers offer lots of opportunities for coverage of a local story. Crucially, they also offer practice in handling the media – for when you become a national celebrity! The approach taken is often much gentler than on the nationals,

---

2 Source: Book Marketing Limited, *Books and the Consumer*, Market Research Report

with the interviewer seeking to coax an interesting discussion rather than ask questions you don't want to answer. What is more, many local radio stations are happy to run a short competition at the end of a feature, with listeners asked to phone in with the answers. This can substantially extend the coverage of your product, and consequently its memorability and eventual sale. Don't think local just means where you live. You may attract coverage where you grew up, used to live, or now work. Most local papers love a 'local boy/girl made good' story.

How long should your list of contacts be? Don't worry if it is long – but don't send a free copy to everyone; if you do so you may erode the basic market of the book. Instead, circulate a press release with information on the book offering a free ('review') copy for those who offer to feature it. The more expensive the title, the more limited will be the review list, but journals may still announce publication even if they do not provide a detailed review.

Achieving publicity and keeping your profile high

Have you noticed that certain politicians and 'television personalities' (whatever that means) are always being quoted? This is not because they sit at home waiting for the telephone to ring; it is usually because they have actively pursued notoriety, sent opinions to programmes seeking sound-bites, and not been afraid to be controversial. In other words, they went in search of opportunities rather than waiting for them to turn up! Don't be intimidated by the idea of this. Remember that the very fact that you have a book being published implies determination (few authors are accepted by the first publishing house they approach), conviction (to have written a book in the first place), and self-confidence (why else would you assume that everyone wants to hear your opinion and that it deserves a wider audience?). What is more, having written a book makes you interesting to the media – there is an assumption that if you are an author, you know something. See chapter 10 for ideas on raising your profile.

Database management

If you are going to self-publish, then there are two lots of names and addresses you will need to look after carefully. The first comprises journalists, commentators and reviewers who may talk about what you publish; the second, customers who may buy it. Care is needed with both groups.

Journalists first. Print off names and addresses and compile a card index for your desk, or maintain a database on your computer. Make a note of what has been said after each call. Accuracy is essential; most people hate their name being mis-spelt, and want you to remember their individual interests.

As regards your customers, an awareness of where the market is and how to approach it is the genesis of many a decision to self-publish, but be aware that database management of the information you hold is very time-consuming and feels much less creative than the act of writing. This probably works best when the book is marketed to a customer database related to the subject of the book (for example, an expert on antiques keeping a list of all the customers to his shop and then writing the definitive book on buying for his customers), but be aware that:

- Managing a database takes time, immense attention to detail and constant updating

- You need to be aware of legal restrictions on the data you hold (most countries have a form of data protection legislation administered by a registrar)

- You will need to invest in computer hardware on which to hold your contacts, buy software to make retrieving them possible, and explain to others how to extract information so that it can be done if you go under a bus

- Data management must be an ongoing concern. For example, all the information you send out must have a return address so that 'gone aways' can be noted as such; you must be aware of duplication to avoid loading the same person more than once (very irritating and looks wasteful) but this is difficult to spot if people register themselves in their own and their maiden name, and use house names and numbers interchangeably. You may come to resent the time you have to spend on the database and thus cannot spend writing.

Order fulfilment

If you do persuade customers to send you money for your books, who will fulfil these orders? Will having to pack up parcels get in the way of writing? Remember that books are easily damaged and heavy to post, and high standards will be expected – no one wants to receive damaged goods. As proof of this, watch customers choosing paperbacks in a bookshop – they may flick through a copy on display, but that will not be the one they take to the till point.

You may decide you want to appoint a distributor. Look in trade magazines for details of organisations offering such services; they may run a regular feature on distribution, and all those interested advertise. Be aware that:

- There are many more publishers wanting a decent distributor than organisations offering to be one
- You will have to pay heavily for the privilege, and pass on a percentage of sales made which have been secured through your efforts, not theirs
- You will probably deem it worth it if you get access to their rep force and they handle the areas you suddenly realise you know nothing about (for example, despatch of export orders and VAT).

Case Study

Chris Perkins

I became interested in coins when I was about eight, when my Uncle Peter gave me some Russian kopek, and I have remained so ever since. I like to think this was never in a nerdy way (perhaps I'm in denial!); I have always been interested in buying and selling things and even dealt in coins and stamps at school. Everyone used to say I could become a great sales-man, but to be honest I never really liked pressuring people who clearly were not interested (later on I was actually a door-to-door canvasser for a short time, but I didn't waste time on people who simply were not interested). My claim to fame from my school years is that I once sold blackberries to a woman whose own garden had unwittingly provided the fruit!

To someone with a natural interest in the past, there is something very appealing about studying and collecting coins. They have passed through the hands of so many people and you are holding pieces of history, and I find it interesting how coins were also used to spread propaganda; putting out the image that the ruler wants others to see. The royal families of Europe and in fact the history of much of the world can be traced back through the little metal tokens that people used for small transactions. Each coin has its own story.

People collect coins in lots of different ways, and usually tend not to be in competition with each other; they are often helpful towards other collectors and can be a talkative com-munity – which of course helps me. Some look for complete sets of all the coin denominations for a particular year; others, for runs of sequential years for a specific denomination. Others collect the coins of a particular reign, country or government, or just all they can find of a particular denomi-nation such as the gold sovereign or silver sixpence.

Whenever major coinage changes occur, and people no longer receive the coins they were previously familiar with in their change, the dealers receive much more interest. So decimalisation in the UK in 1971 and the arrival of the Euro in 2002 were both events that stimulated demand for the older defunct coins – and if Britain goes into the Euro, that will give the business a boost too (but at what price?!).

I was involved with coins as a professional coin dealer for a couple of years, and then Richard Marles, the publisher of a couple of books on the subject under his name 'Rotographic', told me that he was going to sell the rights to his titles and name and then retire. Knowing absolutely nothing about publishing, but having been a reader of his main title (*Collectors' Coins Great Britain*) since the late 80s and seeing a potential in it, I decided to buy the rights and name from him. I bought the list in 2004 and published my first edition, the 32nd, in 2005. It rather appealed to me that my first publishing enterprise was in fact the 32nd edition of a book!

I made many changes to the book, increasing the amount and structure of the information in the book, and how it looked through improving the binding and the quality of the paper. But whereas he had sold it mainly through bookshops, and had no mailing list at all, I reckoned it would be a good idea to sell it direct as well. In particular I planned to promote it through my website, in the hope that people would buy it from me and recommend it to others. Another important thing was that I wanted to be involved in e-books right from the start. E-books are increasingly popular, so I ensured that each of the books I produced was also generated as an indexed digital version to be sold for about 30 per cent less than the printed edition. I now sell a number of e-books each week. The best thing about e-books is that once you've produced it and have the infrastructure in place to offer the buyers the ability to download it, all you need to do is wait! No postage, no wrapping, no storage space and no time (apart from the initial promotion) is required to sell an e-book.

There are two UK coin magazines, and the main one would

not let me advertise in their pages because they saw me as a competitor. Apparently, despite all the anti-competitive practices and legislation we hear about, they are entitled to do that.

'If a magazine sees an author as a direct competitor they can refuse to allow him to advertise. Magazines usually have a complete discretion as to who advertises in their pages.'

Nicola Solomon; Finers, Stephens, Innocent
(experts in the law relating to publishing)

I tried an expensive advertisement in an obscure section of a national newspaper but that brought only one sale! I also put an advert in a more general collectors' magazine but the sales generated were not huge – certainly not enough to cover the cost of the advert. Something that was more successful (mainly because it was cheaper to do) was the insertion of mail-shots in a mass mailing of the British Numismatic Society, of which I am a member.

Sales have to be generated pro-actively; no one else will do it as well as the publisher/author in the case of my main book. I have a background in IT so was able to set up an effective website. I encourage correspondence through my website and my buyers to talk to each other in the forum that I host, and I know that they recommend the book to all new members. I try to change and add content often so there are reasons to return, and have made it as interesting and attractive as possible. I structure the website very carefully so that it is search-engine optimised and therefore easily found by people searching for coin-related key words. In fact, I could probably write a long essay on the subject of search-engine optimisation, which is a hugely complex subject and is something that a lot of people and businesses do not use to their advantage.

The previous owner had sold books to the major high street bookshops, but just because he did, didn't at all mean that the orders would flood in automatically! So, I bugged the retail stores to get them to stock the book. I contact WH Smith, Waterstone's, Bertrams and Easons annually – and anyone else

I think might stock my books. I try to get a name and then follow up a phone call with emails (many companies seem to have email addresses in the format of firstname.lastname@company.co.uk, so I have in the past even been able to guess correct email addresses!). I don't pester too often, but hopefully enough to get me noticed. I send every potential major stockist a free copy so they can see the quality of what I am producing. I try to point at previous sales and assure them that if they stock my books, they will be sold, as there really is a demand. Waterstone's have now made some of my books core stock items, which may sound odd to someone who knows nothing about coins, but there are a lot of collectors out there, and my book benefits all kinds of coin collectors, whatever their interests or shape of their current collection. My main book also allows collectors to value what they own for insurance purposes, so they really need an updated copy each year. Promoting the book myself through the website direct to the reader also brings retail sales to those who stock the books, as many would rather buy a book in a bookshop than through the post.

I do take stands at a limited number of coin fairs and also sell through coin shops, shops that sell metal detecting equipment and the odd antique/bric-a-brac shop. The problem with smaller outlets is the time involved – it takes the same time for me to deal with an order of ten books as it does an order of 1,000, so I think naturally I concentrate sales offensives on the customers likely to buy the most books. The smaller sellers certainly don't get neglected, though.

Another strategy is to produce other related titles, and I currently publish six, with other history and collectable related books in the pipeline. Cross-selling other titles gives me more to offer both my suppliers and my customers, and it also means I can promote the other titles on the back covers of each of the books.

Over the last two years I have grown to quite like publishing. I expect that I may have felt differently had I not had a measure of success (so far, 19,000 books sold in exactly two years)! I like the prestige. I like to tell people 'I'm a publisher' when they ask me what I do. It has a certain satisfying mystique, as they look me up and down and try to judge if I publish classical literature, comics, porno mags or anything in-between! I don't think I could bear going back to having a boss and not being in full control of my own destiny, through nothing but my own hard work and a little luck.

One of the best things about running my business is that I fully embrace the Internet and can pretty much do it wherever I want. Having got fed up with the travel and commuting in and out of London, I went to live with my girlfriend in Germany from where I run my enterprises.

Chris Perkins, www.rotographic.com and www.predecimal.com

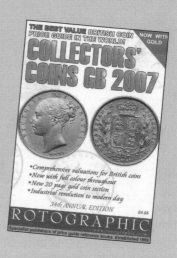

Case Study

Emma Lee-Potter

'You're mad,' said a writer from *The Bookseller* when I told her that after having three adult novels published by Piatkus, I'd decided to self-publish a children's novel called *The Rise and Shine Saturday Show*.

Maybe. But I was drawn to the idea by the thought that I'd be in control of the whole project – not just writing the book, but commissioning a cover, choosing the typeface and even marketing it. I'd had a couple of near-misses with the book and got so fed up with waiting for publishers to get back to my agent that I decided to go it alone. I'd written the book for my daughter Lottie and in memory of my mother, columnist Lynda Lee-Potter, so it also felt like a real labour of love.

The project turned out to be a steep learning curve – but not an insurmountable one. I found that most people, from my printers – Cox & Wyman in Reading – to my typesetters – Hope Services in Abingdon – were incredibly helpful, and happy to fill the huge gaps in my publishing knowledge.

I was determined to have a really pretty cover that would appeal to 9–12 year olds and was delighted to find a talented young student called Meng-Chia Lai, who'd recently won a major illustration award. But one huge mistake was to commission the design before I'd made key decisions – like the size of paperback (B format), the width of the spine, my publishing logo and where the barcode should be. These all had to be added on later down the line so I'd done everything the wrong way round!

As a journalist I was pretty confident that I'd be able to write a snappy press release and get the book mentioned in the press, but clueless about how to get an ISBN number and persuade shops to stock my books.

I decided to get 2,000 copies printed – the minimum the printers would do and the maximum I could store in my house. Some people said I should use a fulfilment company to send out the books but I wanted to keep my costs down to the minimum. I reckoned that if I could sell 1,000 I'd be in profit.

I had proof-read my book over and over again but I knew it was important to get other people to cast their eye over it for typos, accuracy and continuity. My sister and daughter both read it and so did journalist Josa Young. I'd contacted Josa by email after reading a piece in the *Evening Standard* about her own self-publishing project, and even though we've never met we agreed we'd both proof-read each other's novels. It worked brilliantly and we are still in touch!

When it came to writing a press release I made a huge list of everyone I thought might be interested. I knew national newspapers don't have much space to review children's books, so as well as sending copies out to them, I focused on local papers (in all the areas I had ever lived), the trade press (as I'm a journalist I figured that *Press Gazette* and the *Hold The Front Page* website might be interested) and children's magazines. I wrote a carefully tailored press release for each one and it really worked. For the local press I focused on my local connections, while for children's magazines I concentrated on the fact that the book is set in a children's talent show and was being launched to coincide with the new series of *The X Factor*. This approach worked well and in fact BBC Radio Four's children's programme *Go 4 It*, featured the book too, which was great. The one piece of marketing advice I'd give to other self-publishers is to get a decent photograph of yourself taken. When you send out a press release, local papers in particular often ask you to email a picture too and at first I didn't have one of sufficiently high quality.

I also wrote several features about the book for my own website, www.emmaleepotter.co.uk. I mentioned it in my regularly updated blog, posted the first chapter of the book online and offered readers the chance to win a signed copy. I joined the Amazon Advantage scheme, where publishers can sell their books, and also had postcards of the book cover printed to send out to friends and work contacts.

As the book is for children I've focused a lot on local

schools. Several schools invited me in to go and talk to pupils about the book, and writing and journalism in general, and I've done very successful signings afterwards. This has also been a great way of getting feedback from the age group the book is aimed at.

Selling to the retail book trade has been the hardest part of the process. My local bookshops have been supportive and Waterstone's have included the book on their list, but I haven't got anywhere with chains like Borders and WH Smith. As I'm a one-man band and have to do everything myself I've simply focused on other avenues instead. It does feel difficult ringing up bookshops and introducing yourself as both the writer and the publisher, but you've just got to do it. A novelist friend suggests using two different names but I haven't so far.

Three months on, I'm still learning as I go along but the books are selling and I haven't regretted it for a moment. Children have sent letters saying they love the book and I'm now busy writing a follow-up.

The Rise and Shine Saturday Show by Emma Lee-Potter.
Published by Porthminster Press, price £5.99
Find out more at www.emmaleepotter.co.uk

Case Study

Jo Westwood, BA, C. Psychol., Educational Psychologist, Englishtype Ltd & Zed Project

When I decided to spend my time writing some books to help children through the first stages of reading and writing using structured phonics (now often called 'Synthetic Phonics'), I thought that the most difficult part would be in creating interesting stories using a very restricted vocabulary. But that bit of what I wanted to do, although very difficult, was part of my professional expertise, because I had been diagnosing and teaching dyslexic people for some years as an Educational Psychologist, and I knew how to provide a strong structure for effective learning.

The first versions were illustrated by a friend. I had met him as a client; he was dyslexic himself and he had a dyslexic son, whom I had taught to read and write using my methods. We produced versions of the stories (using a photocopier and coloured paper) which could be tested out in schools and then we approached all the educational publishers we thought were relevant (probably 12–15 in all). We had a few interviews with potential publishers – Ladybird, Hodder and Stoughton, Blackie and Heinemann – but every time we were told that structured phonics was out of fashion (the fact that it was then no longer being taught in schools is the reason why we have so many illiterate young people and adults!). Meanwhile, the photocopied 'books' I had made out of our materials were used to destruction in a couple of schools to whom I had given them for trial. I knew that they were effective in helping children to learn to read.

Some time later, I met Lucy Juckes through her mother-in-law, Patience Thomson (I knew Patience from the time we both served on committees at the British Dyslexia Association, and I had had a fruitful association with her in publishing some software). At the time Patience and Lucy were setting up Barrington Stoke to publish children's books, and Zed Project seemed to be a possibility for them to publish. Lucy helped me to find an illustrator, and after a revision of the content of the books in line with what I had learned from the first versions, it seemed that Zed Project would at last become a reality. But then Barrington Stoke decided that they would specialise in books for older children and so Zed was, once again, put to one side. But Lucy suggested that the content was so unusual and effective that it was worthwhile self-publishing. Attempting that was a fast learning curve, but with Lucy's support and access to a printing company owned by a friend, Zed Project became a reality. The day I first saw the books, beautifully illustrated and ready for the children to learn from, I cried. I was intensely proud of what I had achieved. I set up a Limited Liability company, organised the ISBN numbers for the titles, none of which I had ever done before.

With hindsight, I can now see that the difficulties I had encountered in the writing, testing, illustrating and creating the pages, registering them properly and setting up the company were in fact the easy parts. Little did I know how difficult the next stage was to be ...

I have been selling software for more than 25 years and we have a successful company selling touch-typing software. I had thought that my knowledge and experience of marketing software would lead to being able to sell books. I knew about what should be in the books, I relied upon my intuition and knowledge of children to produce books which looked really attractive to them and teachers, but my knowledge of marketing books was zero.

My daughter, Sue, joined our family businesses at the start of 2005. Her academic background is in Psychology, but she had followed a 12-year career working in marketing departments of some of the UK's big-name companies: Cadbury, Unilever, Carlsberg. She decided she wanted to try and sell something more meaningful than beer and chocolate! So, she came on board to work with us and we have had a very enjoyable two years working together. We mostly agree with each other about business decisions – but when we disagree, we always end with a hug to make sure mother and daughter stay in our most important roles! She has increased our software sales by about 50 per cent, a huge achievement in a market that is struggling, and I am immensely proud of her. The books, however, have been a problem – even for her.

Applying her commercial knowledge to the books, Sue set out to look for marketing opportunities, but found that, sadly, the book market is very different from the software market. Lots of software is sold to schools and homes through independent, third-party retailers; effectively a supermarket (in reality, more of an Argos!) for software. This means that independent sellers have an effective means of selling into schools, as well as the very big publishers. All the products sit alongside each other in a catalogue or on the website.

For books, the distribution system seems to be completely linked to the big publishers – there are few independent resellers, and those that there are concentrate mainly on bigname companies and books. We approached the few that we could find, but got absolutely no joy in getting listings in their catalogues. Given that our product was mostly educational in focus, we concentrated efforts here and did not attempt to tackle the high street.

In today's world of technology, the self-publishing part is actually the easy bit. Finding a route to buyers (a distribution channel) and communicating with those buyers so that they are aware of the product is the biggest challenge when it comes to books. One channel that should make all this possible, you would imagine, is the Internet. Here anyone can set up a website to communicate with potential customers, and sell in a virtual shop via that site. It does work to some extent, but the reality of the vastness of the Internet, and the millions of products that are now offered upon it, means that unless you have a very specific product designed for a very specific target, it is likely to be difficult for people to find your site and product. So, sadly, selling books seems to be a tricky business.

Summary of this chapter

Perhaps this chapter has made you realise that there is more to being a publisher than is at first evident. An effective publisher brings to each author:

- experience
- confidence
- contacts.

You may decide it is preferable to get on with what you do best (writing), and delegate the above to the professionals. Alternatively, you may decide to go it alone. Whatever you decide, if the book is to be a success, someone must address the considerations listed at the very beginning of this chapter.

9

Working with your publisher

Good communication between author and publishing house is the best way of producing effective marketing for the forthcoming book. So, whether your path to the publishing house has been relatively straightforward, has been punctured by specific and cruel instances of maltreatment by the house you are now required to work with, or you have been turned down by hundreds of publishing houses and are absurdly grateful to now be offered a contract by this one, put the past behind you. The best results will be achieved by working methodically with this publisher, not re-fighting old battles.

Given that:

- No other industry produces as many new products a year, or offers its employees so little time (or money) with which to market them, and
- All books receive basic attention (catalogue entry and advance notice, information on the database),

your aim is to ensure that you get the maximum possible in-house attention and consequently the best possible resulting sales.

Why do you want to be published?

Spend a few minutes thinking about this rather obvious question. It will help you establish priorities. For example, do you want this book to be published:

- Because you have a burning desire to write, and your career as a writer depends on being published?

- To support other activities such as lecturing or training or your general professional development; a book gives credibility to your wider profile?

According to the rationale provided above, you may be looking for a variety of different kinds of support from your publisher. For example, as a new fiction author you might want the publishers to help with:

- Listing in their promotional materials and linking you with appropriate other (and better known) authors, for example 'the new Joanna Trollope'
- Finding a suitable endorsement for your title from someone well-known, which will encourage the possibly interested to pick up your book
- Leaflets to hand out if you undertake speaking engagements
- A cover blurb and cover that really appeal to the market
- Inclusion in relevant trade promotions, for example Christmas catalogues
- Enthusiastic presentation to the reps with anecdotes, to ensure that they remember your title and pass on the right information to get it stocked in shops.

If your book supports a training course, you might want the publishers to help with:

- Flyers to hand out when training
- An attractive bulk purchase deal to allow you to sell your title as part of training packages
- Very efficient delivery of the same so you can rely on them to get the books where and when they are needed
- Relevant advertising in professional magazines
- Inclusion in direct marketing promotions aimed at the right market
- Liaison with book retailers active in this market

- A cover and blurb that reinforce the image you are trying to create, and appeal to the market.

The author's publicity form[1]

Most publishers send this out at about the same time as you receive your contract (but if you don't get one, do ask). This is your main chance to impress on the publisher the various reasons why they agreed to publish your book. You will be asked for information on what you have done and how that relates to the title planned; to provide a short 'blurb' (written description for promotional purposes) about yourself and the book; and to provide any other relevant information.

It's surprising how many authors fail to fill this form in – almost certainly because they are being asked for information that they have provided before. Take your time to fill it out and answer all the questions. Never just attach a CV and leave the person at the other end to sift through for the information they need. Even worse, please don't write (as I've witnessed): 'I've already told your editorial director, kindly consult him/her' or, even worse, 'This is your job, you tell me'. Remember that the marketing person dealing with your book will be handling lots of other titles simultaneously; if information about you and your book is difficult to find, they may give up the struggle. This is a key promotional platform, so make the best possible use of it.

Fill it out legibly – print or type rather than hand-write, and keep a copy. Be specific. Give precise details of conferences at which you will be speaking, with the dates, venues and the organisers' contact numbers (email and phone). Don't just give the initials of societies – which will almost certainly mean nothing to someone who is not active in the field – and approximate dates.

---

1 Or author's information form. The title may vary, but the document is standard in the publishing industry. See also page 29 and pp. 117–19.

Christopher Helm Publishers Ltd / A & C Black
38 Soho Square, London W1D 3QZ
tel: 020 7758 0022
fax: 020 7758 0222
email: vatkins@acblack.com

Author Publicity Questionnaire

It will help us to promote sales of your book if you would fill in the answers to the following questions and send them to us as soon as possible. Please email the form back to us when complete. If you prefer, print it out and fill it in by hand, posting it to us when complete. The information you give us will provide the basis of you book's promotion in the form of press releases, seasonal catalogues and leaflets etc.

We appreciate that some of the questions may not be applicable to your book, so please do not feel bound by the exact wording of the questions, and expand any answers onto further lines where necessary.

Book Title (including subtitle)
Book title: Talking to Goldfish

subtitle   and listening to their answers

Edition: 1st

Author/Editor/Artist (if your name is ever mispronounced, please indicate the correct pronunciation)
author: Ambrosia Pheenne (pronouced Fin)

Date of Birth (this information is required for some awards eligibility)
Date of birth: 12.11.57

Nationality   Scottish

Address   23 Spottiswoode Close, Edinburgh EH11 1BG, Scotland

Tel. No: 0131 228 5444

Email address: Ambrosia.Pheenne@btopenworld.com

1) A brief biographical sketch including anything relevant to the writing of the book.
A lifelong goldfish lover, I was inspired to write this book by my tenth goldfish Bertie. Having lost my job, I spent far more time in my flat than is usual and suddenly realised that he was consciously mouthing at me. I imitated his movements and conversation began. We have been communicating ever since. Neighbours were fascinated by the tale, it got passed onto our local paper, and I was persuaded that others would find this helpful. This book is the result.

2) Please list professional bodies, organisations, clubs etc of which you are a member.
I am a founder member of the Bruntsfield Acquatic Guild which has an extensive membership.

3) Have you published other books with us or other publishers? Please give titles, publishers, dates.

Accounting for Beginners, Heinemann 1987; *More Accounting for Beginners*, Heinemann 1993; *Accounting for the slightly more experienced*, Heinemann 1995. I have written many academic papers on accountancy for professional journals.

4) Please write a short synopsis of your book (approx 150–200 words) including a summary of the contents which could form the basis of a book jacket blurb.

This is a complete guide on how to communicate with your goldfish. Humans and fish coexist but often take no notice of each other. This book provides step by step guidance on how to get the most out of the relationship. A fish's perspective on your life is absorbing and original – you would be surprised by what they notice – and your views on what it feels like to live out of water are equally interesting to them.

The book includes full guidance on mouth movements and appropriate accompanying noises to attract your fish's attention and ensure a two way dialogue.

5) For lack of space your book may sometimes have to be described in a sentence. What is the shortest statement you can make which aptly expresses its scope and theme?

Communicate with the goldfish in your life, in five easy stages.

6) Please list the main selling features of the book, who you hope will buy it, and why.

This is a completely new book. To my knowledge no one else has written on the same subject. I find that the idea of talking to a fish appeals not only to all goldfish lovers, but also to those who have in the past thought of owning a fish but dismissed the idea as boring. I give unique insight into whether or not goldfish are happier in the company of other goldfish – or humans.

7) Are there any competing books? Please name them and explain how your book differs from them.

None. There was a professor in Lithuania who has given talks on the subject but he is now dead. No one is thought to have been passed his secrets before he died.

8) Are you willing to give press, radio and TV interviews?

Yes.

9) Would you be willing to write (an) article(s) for the press on a subject related to the book?

Yes.

10) Have you any objection to your address or telephone number being given to media wishing to contact you direct?

Yes, please vet all calls before passing them to me. Some people to have a very unhealthy interest in communicating with fish.

11) Is there any particular aspect of your book which may be of special interest to the media?

I think the whole thing is captivating.

12) Have you any personal contact with people who might commend your book or promote the sales? (Media, librarians, booksellers etc). Please give name, position, organisation address and telephone number where possible. Edinburgh papers and broadcast media.

My sister is a librarian, a friend of mine runs a bookshop which would take copies. Contact details on the attached sheet. The BBC programme 'Animal Hospital' should feature my book and Rolf Harris should be sent a personal copy.

13) Are there any regional, specialist or foreign publications to which you think review copies should be sent? Please give addresses where possible. I am told that the former newsreader Martyn Lewis is fond of cats so my have a passing interest in how they relate to goldfish.

14) Are there any areas or particular town where local publicity and bookshop displays might be helpful? Please list these and give reasons. I was born in Berwick upon Tweed and lived there until 10 years ago. Before that I lived in London.

15) Do you ever make visits to schools, libraries etc for book weeks? I give talks in a local primary school during book week.

16) Can you suggest the names and addresses of societies or associations which might help to promote sales of the book, eg by undertaking the distribution of leaflets, or by supplying mailing lists or publishing a journal? Also websites. Give a contact name where possible. I could include a flyer in the next mailing to members of the Bruntsfield Acquatic Guild as I am now the Honorary Chairperson. You should contact the membership secretary Harriet Smart on 0131 228 5628. www.bruntsfieldaquatic.co.uk

17) Is there any particular season or event, to which you think publication should be linked? (conferences, exhibitions etc) Most fish get bought in the autumn.

18) Are there any academic, educational or professional institutions or courses that could use your book? Please give details including addresses where possible. I think my book should be recommended reading for all courses in veterinary medicine.

19) Is the book of any special interest overseas? Which countries? Applicable worldwide, but avoid countries where goldfish are eaten.

20) Further suggestions

As an A&C Black author, you are entitled to buy your own or any title published by us at trade terms, which means in most cases 35% discount (*Who's Who* 25%); payment has to be made within 30 days, and cannot be offset against your royalty account. Postage is free within the UK, or at your cost if outside the UK. We hope you will take advantage of this facility, whether for professional use or as presents. Orders should be sent to: Trade Manager, A&C Black (Publishers) Ltd., PO Box 19, Cambs PE19 3SF.

A meeting with your publisher to discuss marketing

Your contract will specify a date for delivery of the manuscript, and (usually) a planned publication date. About six months before publication it's a very good idea to get in touch with your editorial contact to talk about progress – by this stage the manuscript is most likely nearing the end of the editing process. Even if it is not suggested, this is also the ideal time to ask to meet the marketing person who will be responsible for promoting your book.

Some useful background tips for this meeting

Your attitude and tone of voice will be what is remembered from this meeting, irrespective of how many good ideas you come up with. Before you arrive, remember that you are meeting your publishers, who are investing in you. However frustrated you may feel, if you imply that you would do a better job yourself if only you had the time, and have little respect for their abilities, you will not get the best long-term results.

Never assume that whatever information you have sent in about yourself and your book has either been circulated or fully read. Take another copy and mark the most important points.

Bear in mind that most publishers make a conscious effort to cut down on what they have to read: there is simply too much of it. With manuscript submissions, strategy reports, CVs sent in speculatively by those wanting a job, in-house newsletters and many other documents competing for their attention, your information must stand out. So, use a highlighter pen to draw attention to key parts of your message, use cartoons, or paste on headlines from tabloid newspapers. Above all, never forget that you are selling yourself to your publisher, long after they have agreed to publish your book.

The first meeting

1 **Smile and shake hands**. Be positive and enthusiastic. Ask to meet everyone involved. You may be introduced to the head of the relevant section, but ask to meet those who will actually be doing the work on your book, irrespective of seniority. Ask for

their business cards (most people have them but rarely get to hand them out) and remember their names when you call. Be warned too that publishing employees can rise very quickly – from Marketing Assistant to Marketing Director in as little as four or five years. If you insist on speaking only to the chief, you may be storing up resentment from someone who will very soon be important.

2 **Make no assumptions.** You cannot assume that everyone you meet has read your book. Your commissioning editor is probably the only person you can rely on to have done so, and even then, the copy-editing will almost certainly have been done by someone else. It follows that all those who make decisions that affect the look of your book, and its marketing, need key information on what kind of title it is. The book jacket design and the blurb on the back of the book are generally agreed to be the two most important factors influencing purchase in bookshops; it is therefore important that the person who is briefing the designer and the copywriter understands what they are writing about.

The person responsible for marketing your book will not necessarily understand its subject matter. Indeed, the more specialised the subject matter, the less likely this will be. Publishing attracts many more recruits with an arts background than a science background; it's very common for high science titles to be handled by those with an arts education, and even those with relevant subject experience will often find themselves matched for their personality traits (for example, their ability to get on with difficult authors) or marketing/publishing skills rather than their relevant degree.

This is not necessarily a problem. The marketing person's role is to understand who the market is, where to find them and how to approach them; it doesn't necessarily follow that they start off with any background knowledge of that market. The best way for them to gain this is to ask you lots of questions, but don't assume that if they ask none they understand everything. They may be wary of admitting how little they know, and worry that if you knew this you might dismiss their ability to do the job – usually a mistake. I began my working life in publishing, with a degree in mediaeval history and fine arts, but over the years have success-fully marketed high-level science, medicine and very specialised journals. When working on titles whose subject matter I knew little or nothing about, I often found I did a better job as I was forced to think about who would buy it, rather than relying on out-of-date hunches based on inadequate knowledge.

Not everyone you meet will have read your author publicity form. Publishers are very bad at bureaucracy. Never assume that a letter you sent has completed the circuit of all who are possibly interested/involved. So, take along a copy to the meeting, and provide a list of bullet points updating those you meet on what you have been up to since. Remember that in addition to looking after your book, the marketing staff may have to come up with plans for 20–30 other titles during the same month, so if the information you provide is easy to use, it is more likely to be acted upon.

What to establish at your first marketing meeting with the publisher

A word of warning before you arrive: remind yourself to listen. You are a writer; you are supposed to be good at picking up the nuances in relationships and conversations. If you fire questions at them, you will alienate them. But by listening and trying to pick up the signals, you should emerge from this first meeting with information that will answer, at least in part, most of the following questions.

- What kind of title will this be? Is it a key title (the jargon is 'lead title') or just one of the many they are publishing that season ('mid-list')? You will get a feel for this by the seniority of the staff involved in your meeting. (Titles that have passed their first peak of sales but, rather than going out of print, have passed into the house's standard list of titles available, are known as 'back list'.)

- How long is the payback period for the publisher's investment? How many books do they intend to have sold by various points in the future (say three and six months, two and five years)? How long do they anticipate it will remain in print for? Do they anticipate a need to update it in a few years time? Is it part of a growing imprint or a completely new venture for them? You may be surprised to know that your contract with the publisher will very seldom include an indication of how many copies they are likely to print. (They may tell you, if you ask.)

- What is the timing for publication, and is this of particular importance? Publishing is a very seasonal business. New editions of textbooks for use in schools and colleges must be available in time to announce them for the academic year ahead. Most literary novels are launched in time for the key autumn buying and stocking season that prepares for Christmas. Once they are in the shops, timing remains crucial. A mass-market novel may have as little as six weeks in the shops before it is either reordered or sent back to the publishing house for a credit; children's titles may take years to get established. It follows that the timing of the marketing and publicity for books is particularly sensitive – the marketing must be timed to produce demand just at the time when the books are in the shops ready to be sold. All of which means that it's important to deliver your manuscript on time.

- How much money will be spent on marketing your book? Will the book be marketed on its own or in combination ('piggy-backed' or 'cooperatively') with other books from their list? Most publishers try to build a reputation as a particular kind of house with strengths in certain areas, so cooperative marketing is not necessarily a disadvantage if it means you reach more people by pooling the sums that might have been spent on titles individually.

- Is any direct marketing planned? In which case, do you have key contacts that you could contribute to the mailing list? What societies or organisations do you belong to? Could information be included in one of their regular mailings? Bear in mind the regulations covering data protection: you can't just send your publisher a copy of your child's class list and ask them to mail all the parents.

- What about promotional activity? Lots of magazines and newspapers feature 'reader offers' these days to boost loyalty. Can you think of any such media that might be particularly interested in your book? What other items do you buy on a regular basis that might make a useful link? For example, mail order catalogues sometimes use books to boost the size of the order. By organising promotions you may get space at a very competitive rate.

What can you do to help?

- Can you circulate leaflets about your book? Most authors can make use of these – perhaps to hand out if you are speaking, give out at exhibitions or send out with your Christmas cards. Could the publisher provide you with a showcard (a poster or notice on card, often made to stand up and with an appropriate backing like a photograph) to attract attention to the book when you are speaking? Remember that publishers are fundament-ally merchants of ink on paper, so the ease and cost with which they can get printed support materials will be substantially less than you would incur should you do it yourself.

- Would you like stock of the book to sell? Publishers love to know about this, as it helps the economics of publishing your book. Many authors who attend lectures, training seminars or conferences as a speaker take along stock to sell at the same time (or even get their book included in the price paid by dele-gates). They can buy stock for this purpose from the publisher at a trade price (there is usually an extra discount if they buy in bulk) and thus make an additional sum to the royalty on each copy sold. Your contract may specify if you are allowed to do this or not, and if you are, be sure to take along a receipt pad and make it clear that you are offering your books to pur-chasers. Authors are mostly self-employed, and so being able to claim an expense is an additional incentive to purchase.

- Do you have an up-to-date photograph that could be used in publicity material? This does not need to be an expensive under-taking (find out when children in your local school are having their photographs taken, and ask if you can be tagged on at either end of the day). Your publishers may pay for a studio shot for the cover, so you could request copies of the image for use if you are sending information out. If you are having a photo taken by a friend, ensure that it is of a sufficiently high resolution to be used in the press (most aren't).

- Do you have contacts in the media and elsewhere that could be useful? Do you have friends or colleagues that could provide a positive quotation about your book? An endorsement from a third party will be much more valuable to the marketing team than the words they (or you) think up. Trawl through your address book for possible names and contact details to pass on to your publisher. Better still, approach them yourself and submit the details – if your contacts are famous or particularly busy it may be easier for you to approach them directly than to rely on the publishing house to do it.

- Could you assist the publisher's rep force? Find out if the publishing house uses reps, and if so, how they will be involved in selling your book. Could you invite your local rep along to a party in a bookshop? This is always a good way of boosting a relationship between author and publisher! Most publishing houses employ reps to either call on retail outlets, or at least to phone them up on a regular basis. Are there local reps for your area (both where you live and work) that you could be put in touch with? For example, they might be able to organise a signing session or arrange PR in the local paper, or you could invite the rep along to a party you were planning to celebrate publication – such thoughtfulness will be remembered.

- Do you have contacts in the book trade (for example, a friend who runs a bookshop) who could be usefully mentioned to the local rep? Could you provide an interesting theme (or bit of gossip) about writing the book for your editor to pass on to the reps at the sales conference? Many people are fascinated by the process of writing, so passing on the detail of how early you got up, how long you kept going for, or what kind of biscuits sustained you may be interesting to the market. Remember, as with so much marketing, the aim is to be memorable; to ensure that the information sticks in the minds of those who make stocking decisions, as well as those who buy the end product.

A final word on volunteering

Don't offer to do anything that you don't intend to see through. Mentioning that your brother-in-law is a reviews editor on a national newspaper, if you have a family agreement not to mix work and home, is pointless, and likely to lead to frustration. Make a careful note of what you do offer, and see it through.

Case Study

Making useful links to promote your book

A note from Mr Hall, deputy head of Kingston Grammar School, came home with two of our children recently, announcing that Jonnie Leach, a psychotherapist specialising in the treatment of young people (and also a former drug addict), would be speaking to individual year-groups – and that there was an opportunity for parents to hear the same presentation in the evening. I signed up to attend, and then thought it might be a useful opportunity to make available copies of the book I co-wrote on parenting teenagers (*Whatever! A down to earth guide to parenting teenagers*, Piatkus 2005, co-written with educator and trainer Gill Hines).

I wrote back to Mr Hall, asked if it would be possible to make the book available on the night, and offered to send a copy of the book both to him and to the speaker before he made his decision. I felt it would compromise both of them if they were asked to offer promotional space to something they had not seen or did not approve of. Mr Hall was happy to proceed. As the audience was to consist of other parents, many of whom I know, I suggested to my daughter and a friend that they might like to run a book stall, offering and selling books, and to keep any profits they made towards their World Challenge Appeal.

Unsurprisingly, given that he lectures on drugs education, Jonnie Leach began reading our book at the chapter on that subject; he loved what he saw and, at the end of the talk,

when asked about what practical steps parents could take to help prevent their children getting into problems, recommended it enthusiastically to the audience. The girls quickly sold all 30 copies; parents wrote out cheques and asked for additional copies to be delivered to school. Since then Jonnie has moved from school to school running more workshops, and enthusing about the book. He is a really proactive ally – one who is changing children's attitudes to drugs all over the country – and (pleasingly for us) promoting our book at the same time.
www.jonnieleach.com

Author etiquette

Endless stories circulate in publishing about which authors are most troublesome to deal with. If you are a sufficiently good writer, and your books are selling well, you can be as awful as you like:

'Be nice or be vile but don't vacillate; I like to know where I am. If the book sells I can put up with you even if you are a shit.'

Andrew Franklin, MD, Profile Books addressing
the Society of Authors AGM, September 2006

As an author, you may see endless opportunities to be critical of your publishing house, but feeling empowered to comment is usually a mistake:

'Be nice. Don't correct the grammar or spelling mistakes in their emails – or if you must, do so in your head, not by return of post.'

Stewart Price, author

Apart from being rude (how would you feel if someone paid attention to your single mistake rather than to the overall thrust of your message), such a response to a marketing person is badly targeted. In general, whilst all publishers tend to be people who care about words, it is the editors who will be most careful about how information is sent out. Marketing staff are a different breed – more inspired by the idea than the format. They are likely to send you a quick email to outline an opportunity; this may be less than perfectly phrased because they are under pressure. If you respond to their enthusiasm by making them feel small, the chances are that you may not be offered another similar opportunity. Most marketing people have too much to do, and are chasing ideas that crop up at the last minute. These may be pursued with more vigour on behalf of authors who respond to their ideas with enthusiasm rather than with pernickety criticism. You have been warned!

Summary of this chapter

When authors get together, they love to talk about the inadequacies of their publishers, with a frequent issue being how little marketing was done/thought of. If just a fraction of that energy were devoted to *working with* the publishers, great things might be achieved.

> 'One of the last things we understand is how we ourselves are perceived.'
> Ebba Haslund, author,
> from *Nothing Happened*

A very common complaint by publishers about authors is that they do not value publishers' time. So ensure that you provide relevant information when it is most useful (nine months pre-publication, not two weeks afterwards) and consolidate your contacts rather than being constantly in touch.

Authors are articulate and can demolish people with words. What a shame if that means the publisher on the receiving end does not want to communicate with them, and good ideas that could boost sales are not taken up because it is simply too much of a risk.

10

How to get publicity

What is publicity?

You will probably have noticed that marketing terminology is used very casually in publishing. In some companies, 'publicity' is a catch-all phrase for marketing activity or staff; in others it may be the specific job of one person. In the context of this chapter, I am talking about publicity as editorial coverage in the media which leads both to promotion by word of mouth and to sales. Publicity is often a subliminal sell: the publicist tries to lodge so many references to a particular project in the brain of the consumer that the latter is prompted to buy the book without ever having formally made the decision so to do.

An important point to grasp is that because publicity strives to achieve editorial space – i.e. to get your project included in a newspaper's features or news coverage, rather than as a paid-for ad – the publicist is effectively asking for something for nothing. At the same time, all media can calculate exactly what the space is worth (from their advertising rates). It follows that in return for the space allocated, the medium chosen will certainly want something in return: a scoop (a story before anyone else has it) or an interesting angle that will appeal to their readers. However, the story they want to feature and the image you want to present may not be the same.

You should also remember that in a publishing context:

* Publicity should communicate with the target market for the title you are promoting, and not be an end in itself. The person who reads a story about an author should also note that there is a book available

- Publicity must be accompanied by information on availability (where and how to buy) for sales to result
- Publicity is not the same thing as public relations; achieving publicity does not always mean gaining positive coverage. But a negative story may generate interest and sales even more effectively than a positive one. Here is an example from the gossip column of *The Daily Telegraph*. One journalist's negative response to a book has been turned into a story:

Back to sender

HELENA Frith Powell's latest book, *Two Lipsticks and a Lover*, has raised eyebrows on both sides of the Channel by exposing the lusts and secret lives of French women through their choice of lingerie.

According to Vanessa Feltz, the book 'incensed British women' by branding them 'scruffy and fat'. And now, I hear that *Woman's*

Weekly has returned a review copy in disgust. 'In 10 years in publishing, I have never seen a journalist return a free copy of a book,' Powell's editor at Gibson Square Books tells me. 'It came with a rather prudish note saying "not suitable for us".' Powell is equally astonished. 'Then again, if they think the book is too saucy for them, that's probably a good thing,' she tells me.

How publicity is orchestrated

Most publishing houses have a publicity department. It does not follow, however, that all authors and books get publicity organised on their behalf. The author who suggests angles that could be exploited, finds media vehicles to be pursued, and is cooperative in the process (without overdoing it and becoming a nuisance), is more likely to obtain the attention of the house publicist. Remember that in any single month it is likely that your publishing house will be promoting at least 30 titles. There is not enough time, energy or resources to go round.

Who does what – publicists and journalists

Publicists deal with journalists, and try to persuade them to cover the author/book they are promoting. They may be working for the house that is publishing the book, or as a hired hand – perhaps employed by a firm of publicity specialists or as a freelance. To get the most out of both publicists and journalists, it may help to know what kind of people you are dealing with. Characteristically (and this is a generalisation), publicists are:

* Eternal optimists – they keep going when rejected
* Good at juggling – they have to deal with lots of different ideas at different stages of development at the same time, and remember where each one is at
* Perhaps less interested in your literary skills than in your ability to attract headlines. Bear in mind that by the time a publicist gets involved, the book has already been commissioned; their professionalism lies in making the media sit up and take notice, not in literary appreciation. So don't be dispirited if they make little reference to your book's merit and concentrate only on its news potential.

If the book is really strong in its own right (great read, won a significant literary prize, first novel that has huge potential) they may be able to generate coverage for your title on its own merits. Even then, the accompanying story will be relevant (think of Zadie Smith and Arundhati Roy – both hailed as wonderful novelists, but their looks and personalities still used extensively in the publicity process).

Again, these are generalisations, but **journalists** are:

* Cynical – they have seen it all before; it's up to the publicist to tempt them with new ideas
* Busy – and with their time at a premium, the more you can do for them, the better (from your point of view) the likely end results. Press releases written in a way that allows a specific journalist to incorporate them immediately will always do better than those made for blanket application

- Distracted – they work in offices where most of us would find it very difficult to concentrate: phones ring, people talk loudly

- Overwhelmed by other people's information: a realisation of just how many press releases a journalist or literary editor gets each day can be very dispiriting

- As Dotti Irving of Colman Getty PR, specialists in the book business, pointed out, they are more inclined to believe each other than the publicist, which is why a feature in a national newspaper can sometimes encourage other papers to pick it up

- Increasingly well-known in their own right:

'The relationship between interviewer and interviewee has changed over the same period [the last 45 years – since he began writing]. What used to be a rather bland and deferential conversation has become more probing and aggressive. Interviewers want blood – the blood of new and personal revelations – in exchange for the free publicity they offer their subjects. They want to assert their own personalities, and to demonstrate their own literary skills. They can become minor celebrities themselves in consequence. The interviewees, on the other hand, are apt to feel wounded and betrayed by such treatment.'

David Lodge, afterword to *Home Truths*, Penguin

What an author can do to help in the publicity process

Be helpful

Accept that publicity is going to help sell the book; decide to cooperate even though personal coverage in mass media is not to your taste. Be prepared to be resourceful about what you have done in the past. The publicist will want you to be as unsqueamish as you can about others digging into it. Here Janice Dickinson responds to a question on why people are fascinated by models – does the profession drive people mad?:

'It's no different from writing or rock 'n' roll or acting. It's the same. You're obviously fascinated with it because you're interviewing me. It's a fascinating subject.'

Janice Dickinson, the self-proclaimed first supermodel,
being interviewed by Metro, 21st September 2006

Be pragmatic

Don't talk about things you are not prepared to discuss with journalists. You will just create frustration.

'The publicist at my publishing house noted that I had dedicated my novel to the memory of a child. She asked for details, which I gave, but I added that this was not something I wanted to be interviewed about. She then seemed to lose interest, as I could see that all other angles were weak by comparison. I wished I had not mentioned it, although perhaps the problem had been created by me; adding the dedication in the first place was bound to raise questions so was probably not wise.'

Author

Be pro-active

Provide a list of your useful contacts, experiences, future plans, and so on.

'As my books have a direct link with particular venues. and appeal to tourists as well as to the local population, I contacted these places and suggested they come on board with school groups and local press. This worked exceedingly well. The only downside has been the huge amount of time involved on my part, but it has meant getting into some interesting places and has led to quite a lot of press coverage and other publicity opportunities.'

Linda Strachan, creator of Hamish the Haggis

Keep in touch

Let your publicist know what you are up to – all snippets of information can be useful. For example, if you are asked to judge a literary prize, or awarded a directorship, your publicist may be able to sell a feature about you on the back of it.

Be realistic

An appearance on Oprah will not be possible for everyone. Very few authors get mass-market advertising.

What makes the ideal author from a publicist's point of view?

In broad terms, a publicist wants to know why you are interesting. For authors – who usually want to be appreciated for their work, not their personalities – this can be a difficult thing to deal with. For a recent seminar organised by the Society of Authors, Tony Mulliken of Midas PR, a company that specialises in working within the publishing industry, helped me with the following list of ten vulgar questions to which a publicist would like to know the answer:

1 What do you look like? Would a photograph of you make journalists sit up and take notice?

2 Are you married/having a relationship at the moment, and with whom? Have you had a relationship in the past that would be of interest to other people?

3 Can you talk as well as write? Would you interview well?

4 What useful contacts do you have?

5 What's dramatic about you? What have you done in the past that could be turned into a useful story?

6 What hobbies, or better still obsessions, do you have that could be made to sound interesting?

7 Who are your enemies? (Controversy can be wonderful for getting publicity.) What kind of trouble have you run into in the past?

8 Would you be willing to write articles for no money?

9 Where do you live and what do your neighbours think of you? Are you willing to open your house up to the media?

10 What is your relationship like with your family? Famous parents can be very useful, as can 'black sheep relations' happy to bring a private dispute into the public domain.

What is the most difficult type of author to promote from a publicist's point of view?

Someone who:

- Sees their book as their final statement and won't add anything to it
- Clams up when confronted by the media
- Complains constantly about what has not been achieved rather than acknowledging the effort that has gone into the process; never says thank you for what has been achieved
- Is immensely suspicious
- Has no sense of humour
- Doesn't respond to media interest immediately – if you delay, they will be onto the next story.

What kind of coverage might you achieve?

There are a number of specific locations in the media that are devoted solely to books (such as the review pages), but don't assume that these dedicated pages are the most important places to start. As Dotti Irving of Coleman Getty PR pointed out, there are vastly more people reading the news pages than the reviews pages! And then there are other opportunities too: sometimes they need ideas for features – preferably those their competitors have not already thought of; at other times you can make a specific pitch for a particular slot. Bear in mind that for each type of coverage, a different journalist is likely to be in charge, so there could be many different people on a particular outlet that you should keep in touch with. Here is some guidance:

- Review coverage – on the books page. *Contact:* the Reviews Editor
- Feature coverage – through a specially commissioned article or interview. *Contact:* the Features Editor

- Specific, regular spots in a paper – for example, 'Life in the Day of' in *The Sunday Times,* or regular programmes/columns such as 'Desert Island Discs', or ,'What's in your fridge?'. *Contact:* each feature would have its own editor

- Diary coverage. *Contact:* find out the name of the piece and address it to the Editor

- Trade press. They will have all the above slots, and probably a 'gossip column' for light-hearted stories, which gets a lot of attention.

Getting the timing right

Effective timing is crucial for achieving publicity. Why?

- Because it takes time to consider how best to secure coverage, to finalise and format your information attractively, for journalists to consider it, for proof copies of the book to be despatched and for the interviews to be arranged

- Because you need to ensure that the publicity appears at the same time as the book is available for purchase, and this takes planning.

In the run-up to publication, the publishing house's reps will (either personally or by telephone) try to persuade bookshops to take stock on the grounds that there will be demand. For this reason it is very important that any associated publicity should peak when the books are available in the shops. Bookshops have a very short period of time over which a book is deemed to be a success (and further stock ordered) or a failure (and stock sent back to the publisher). If the publicity is late, and the demand consequently delayed, the book may already be back with the publisher when the public start to ask for the title, and sales will probably never recover.

It follows that starting to think about publicity when the book comes out is no use at all. Publicity needs to be thought about a good six months before. If an agent is negotiating your publishing contract, a figure to be spent on marketing and publicity is probably agreed then. If you are handling the negotiations yourself, this is something you will have to bring to your publisher's attention at that point. Tony Mulliken again:

'My advice to authors wanting publicity is to rattle the cage, and do so early. The more fuss you make, the more attention you will get.'

How much to rattle the cage is a question of judgement. If you are constantly on the phone you may alienate, but do remind the publicist seriously and proactively about what you think is possible. Try to amalgamate your requests and contacts into reasonable chunks (rather than sending an email every couple of hours) and express them in a tone that combines passion with achievability.

Trying to get publicity for your own books

How to draw up a publicity plan

1 Look at the book/product objectively and think about the options available (which journalists to approach; which media you think most likely to run a story on you)

2 Decide what is achievable based on time and resources

3 Make a list of preferences

4 Make what you send specific. A handwritten note, or letter referring to what you have seen them cover recently, carries a strong message; this person knows what we do and is contacting us directly, rather than as the result of a mass mailing. This is flattering, and more likely to get a positive response

5 Follow them up (by email, post or phone call – although not too often).

How to get the names of journalists

You may be familiar with many names from reading the papers. But these are often either staff or freelance writers who work under the direction of the 'section editor' for a particular area of the paper or programme. It is the section editor who directs what gets written about, and who can commission new features on forth-coming matters of interest to the audience/readership. So how do you get hold of their names? Firstly, you can build your own lists using a copy of a media yearbook. For example, writing yearbooks include the names, addresses and contact numbers for national and local press and broadcast media. If you have time to do a personal mailing piece, you could ring each specific medium and ask for the names of those you wish to contact (checking difficult spellings) and the address (usually email) to which they would like material sent (often not the same as the general address of the paper in question). If you have less time, you could just send your information to the relevant editor by job title at the address given.

Be rigorous in keeping records of those you have spoken to. Which is their day off, when is the best time to contact them? Journalists working on Sunday papers generally have Monday off, but their life becomes very frantic towards the end of the week as publication gets nearer.

Alternatively, there are several media agencies that specialise in maintaining lists of journalists. You can order names by subject specialisation (for example, all journalists dealing with children's products) in a variety of formats (email file, labels, etc.).

What to send out to journalists

- A press release
- A copy of the book, or a proof or 'reading' copy, or the offer of a free copy on request.

How to write a press release

A press release is an information sheet sent to a journalist to try to stimulate media coverage. This is usually achieved in one of two ways:

1 The journalist uses your press release in its entirety, inserting the words you supply into the paper or medium they write for

2 The journalist decides to write or commission a feature based on the information you send in – usually an author interview or an article based on the issues your book draws attention to.

The main point to bear in mind is that most journalists receive hundreds of press releases every day; the more desirable the medium you are pursuing, the more press releases they will receive. The best advice is to:

- Keep it short (a single side of A4 is plenty; readers on a website don't want to scroll down more than twice)
- Divide up the copy with subheadings and into short paragraphs so that it motivates the reader to get involved
- Make it interesting.

The last point is easier said than done. To start with, cut out long sentences of introductory copy about the publishing house and background information on the author (unless strictly relevant). Try to bring the atmosphere of the book to life, or to highlight the issues it raises, rather than give a complete account of the content. For example, is Daphne du Maurier's *Rebecca* the story of a local landowner's second marriage to a much younger woman – or a compelling tale of one woman's jealousy for a dead rival?

Bear in mind too that publication of yet another book is not really news to a journalist – there will be at least 400 other titles published the same day! What the journalist wants is a *story*, so what kind of 'peg' can you offer on which to hang one? This may be something in the book, but equally could be something in your background, or in the news, or a publicity event tied to publication.

Email or paper version?
Both are needed. Most journalists like to receive press releases by email, as the material can then be used immediately, but a printed press release inserted inside books sent out for review can hold attention, particularly if it is visually attractive. Similarly, you should have printed copies of your press release available at any author interviews or publicity events you attend. It can be handed to the producer/manager looking after you. One will probably have been sent ahead, but having it there, at the ready, is helpful.

Other facts to bear in mind when preparing press releases:

- Give your press release a headline, not just the book title. A headline serves to draw the eye in; it does not need to be a complete summary of what follows.

- Put the main facts in the first paragraph (the journalist may get no further, and if the press release does get included whole, it will be cut from the bottom upwards). You have not got time for an eloquent, mood-filled paragraph to set the scene. The former editor of *The Sunday Times*, Harold Evans, said that the opening paragraph should have the 'who, what, where, why and when' made really clear.

- If you are trying to get feature coverage, make the press release specific to the medium you are approaching. For example, a mass market and a highly professional magazine might cover the same book, but the angle taken would be different in each case.

- Ensure that your grammar and spelling are correct, particularly when writing to literary editors. You are writing to people who care about words; if the press release is poorly compiled your readers will assume that the book is of the same standard.

- Do not repeat the book jacket copy in the press release. This looks lazy and is wasting a separate opportunity to communicate with the market.

- Always put a contact name, email address and telephone number at the bottom of the page (it could be someone in the publisher's publicity department, or perhaps your own). If you are available for interview, or could give an explanation/do a stunt that could make a press event, then the press release should say so.

- Try to make the press release visually arresting. Can you include illustrations – perhaps cartoons, an author photograph, a cover shot or an illustration from the book? In a further bid to make what you send stand out, can you print it on coloured paper? If 99 per cent of the postbag is printed in black ink on white paper, a coloured sheet will draw attention to itself.

- Be wary of using quotations on press releases. If you do, it must be clear that they draw attention to the book's great interest and don't imply that every angle has already been thought of. For this reason, at the end of the quotation, give the name of the contributor rather than the medium in which it appeared.

- Don't send press releases out too often or if you don't have particular news to impart: you will devalue your future impact. What is news? Peter Hobday, radio presenter, provided this useful litmus test:

> 'News is something that is unusual enough to be noticed that the reader will want to talk about it to his wife at home or in his local with his mates.'
>
> From *Managing the Message*, Allison & Busby

- An associated freebie can work to attract a journalist's attention. Review copies of *Confessions of a Southern Lady* (Silver Moon Books) were sent out with a (very well packed!) miniature bottle of Southern Comfort. Be very wary of using humour, however – ideas that seem hilarious at 4.55 p.m., just before you go home, can appear very different in the cold light of day when the post is received. A reviews editor commented that finding out the Valentine she had been sent was in fact a publicity stunt to draw attention to a new book made her feel very disinclined to oblige with either interview or feature.

- Provide a picture of the author with a caption. Remember that images with lots of colour are more likely to be used than those with little, and that an interesting photo (with a fascinating caption) is more likely to be used than a photograph showing a line-up of people holding drinks.

Local press

Don't assume that only national media are worth pursuing. Local coverage can be very helpful, as it offers:

- A direct vehicle to a particular market. If a book has a strong regional flavour, or the author strong local connections, try to get coverage in a local paper.

- Less of a hard-nosed approach than the nationals. This gives authors inexperienced with the publicity process the chance to practise dealing with the media.
- Extra opportunities for coverage. These exist where the author was born, went to school or university, where they live now and have lived previously, where their family came from and so on.

What to do if a journalist won't take your calls or never takes up any of your ideas

Don't despair. Get to know the other people working on the desk: even if it is not an extensive department there will almost certainly be a 'number two'. It follows that:

- They get fewer calls, so may be able to talk to you for longer
- If the ideas you suggest are sensible and interesting, they are a direct route to the main editor. Their voice behind an idea you suggest will have more weight than your own
- One day they will probably be the lead journalist themselves (either on the current slot or elsewhere), and if you have built up good relations you will have someone who will always take your calls.

How to give an effective media interview

An interview with a local radio station is often the starting point for an author's involvement in publicity. The interviewer's approach is unlikely to be aggressive; they will be more concerned with producing interesting listening than extracting a confession you don't want to give. Nevertheless, a few words of advice may be useful.

- Listen to the programme on which you are scheduled to appear for several days before your appointment. Concentrate on the interviewer's style; think about the questions you are likely to be asked and what kind of people are likely to be listening.

- A television programme will give you advice on what to wear (the level of formality required) and usually help you avoid a colour that clashes with the set. If you are preparing for a radio interview, wear clothes that are comfortable, and avoid jangling bracelets. Beware of filling up your glass with water whilst on the air – from the throaty gurgle, the listener may conclude that you are imbibing much stronger stuff!

- When the interview starts you will probably be nervous, so concentrate on listening to the questions asked rather than thinking about what you want to say. If an interview develops as a conversation, this will make you feel much more comfortable and produce more interesting listening.

- Do not prepare a statement to read out. This will sound wooden and unconvincing, and will tempt you to use words that are part of your written rather than your spoken vocabulary (and are therefore harder to understand). What is more, if the statement is part of the press release sent by a publishing house, the interviewer may use it to introduce you. Try to talk from memory, but with the three most important themes (headlines only!) that you must get over, whatever the questions asked, noted down in case your mind completely freezes.

'If the public have to make an effort to understand, they will not make the effort.'
                                        Peter Hobday, radio presenter

- The best preparation is to have thought around the subject-matter of your book, and to have considered the possible questions. Can you get a friend to practise interviewing you so you get used to both the approach and the sound of your own voice? Likely questions include:

  - Why did you write the book?
  - What is the book about?
  - Who will read it?
  - How long did the writing/research take you?
  - What are you planning to do next?
  - What advice do you have for other people who would like to write a book?

- If statistics are central to your argument, have one or two to hand (no more) and try to express them in their simplest form (for example, 'half' rather than '50 per cent').
- Re-read the book just before the interview. This is particularly important if you are now immersed in another project.

Case Study

A new author seeking to support the efforts of her publishing house

Adultery for Beginners by Sarah Duncan

The publicity department understandably concentrates on the major publications with big circulations – magazines and national papers. So they're not that interested in local press, which seems fair enough – it takes as long for them to talk to the editor of the *Denbighshire Free Press* circ 7,000 as the editor of *Heat*. Also they can't possibly know all the minutiae of where you've lived, worked, etc.

I wrote my own press release and tailored it to each town/ city/area I had some sort of connection with. This is easier and less time-consuming than it sounds, but it's important to get the local connections in the first paragraph, and ideally the first line. A friend who's a producer for a local BBC station said that the BBC is strict about the local angle, especially for fiction; with non-fiction they can often come up with their own local angle.

I also had my own photographs taken – if you have them done at commercial rates it's much, much cheaper than 'portrait' shots – and got them on disc. I used the publisher's publicity department as the contact name and phone number on the release. Then I emailed the press release and photographs as attachments to all the relevant newspapers and local radio stations (email addresses found in *Benn's Directory of*

Press at the library). And then I got carried away and did about 100 others.

Ideally I should have followed it up with a phone call the next day, but I didn't have the time. Even so, a lot did 'bite': within two hours of my mass emailing there were three newspapers wanting interviews. Who knows what the impact was on sales? I ended up with a nice file full of clippings which made me feel good!

Using the Internet was so easy and it cost nothing except time – perhaps 1–2 days work in total, what with getting the email addresses, writing the press release and so on. Sending the photographs by email was a godsend as it would have cost quite a lot of money to have them reproduced, and taken about ten days (I'd done it at the last minute) and then there would have been postage. Also, I'm told that newspapers prefer press releases by email as it means they don't have to key them in again.

For my second book, *Nice Girls Do*, my publicist was very enthusiastic and keen, and I was under pressure with the deadline for my next book, so I didn't do any of my own publicity but instead relied on her. The result so far has been lots of reviews in national magazines and newspapers, but no radio interviews at all, and only my local paper has done a feature on me. Writing this two weeks after publication I don't know (yet!) if the lack of local coverage will have an impact on sales – *Nice Girls Do* is currently ninth in *The Bookseller*'s chart; *Adultery for Beginners* reached number three. I'm not concerned, as I think commercial fiction sales are influenced mainly by price discounting and a good cover. But I wish I had been able to spare the time to do more, and intend to do so for my next book.

In my experience, publicity people are charming and optimistic, but overworked and operating on tiny budgets. I've chaired several committees, and the worst sort of member is the one who has lots of bright ideas and high expectations but thinks that someone else ought to do the work and grumbles when nothing happens. I think publicity departments probably feel the same way about authors.

Case Study

Overcoming media resistance

Falling Leaves by Adeline Yen Mah, Penguin

It can be very difficult to achieve publicity for a title that is coming out in paperback, having been launched as a hardback. Many media outlets will not re-review a title that has already been published, however worthwhile. The publicist's second difficulty was to convince journalists that this was an accessible story of human interest that would appeal to a wide variety of people; she feared that on first sight, many would consider it too high-brow or political. As far as women's magazines were concerned, many of the more prominent titles felt that it wasn't UK-based enough to make it viable for them. Finally, as the story happened so long ago, she had to overcome a view amongst editors that this meant there was not enough of a hook for an interview with the author now.

Lydia Drukarz, for Midas Public Relations, says:

'My key objective was to get them to read the press release – once they did that, they were converted relatively quickly. I tried to impress upon the media that this should be considered as a global story of an unhappy and abused childhood, that could equally well apply to any child anywhere, not just in China. This definitely helped secure both the Esther programme (as part of a feature on children who are used as scapegoats) and the interview in *Frank* magazine.

I feel that the review coverage, together with the wide range of television coverage, really helped establish *Falling Leaves* as a bestseller, and brought it to the attention of a real cross-section of the book public.

The book appeals on many levels – firstly as a general human interest story. Then, on the abused childhood angle, it reaches out to those who have been through something similar. Finally it speaks to those readers who appreciate a well-written and gripping story.

In addition to the above, the fact that the publicity campaign was spread out over a period of many months helped to keep the sales buoyant. Adeline first came over to the UK for three weeks. She then came back in August to speak at the Edinburgh Book Festival and to do publicity in Ireland. Whilst in the UK in August, she recorded the *Bookworm* programme, which was finally aired in October. This gave us several opportunities to remind the public that the book was still out there, and kept it in their minds.'

FALLING LEAVES
An Unwanted Chinese Daughter
by Adeline Yen Mah
Published on 2 April in paperback by Penguin Books at £6.99

'I was the ostracized outsider longing for acceptance; the ugly duckling hankering to return as the beautiful swan; the despised and unwanted Chinese daughter, obsessed with my quest to make my parents proud of me on some level. Surely if I tried hard enough to help in dire need, they would love me.'

Although she was born into an affluent and influential family in Shanghai during the 1930s, Adeline Yen Mah was spurned when her mother died giving birth to her, and her father remarried a beautiful yet cruel Eurasian. At the time, her Grand Aunt had formed the Shanghai Women's Bank and her father, having started his own firm at the age of nineteen, was known as the miracle boy with the power of turning iron into gold. Yet in the midst of this wealth, Adeline - the fifth child and youngest daughter - was discriminated against, neglected and emotionally and physically abused by the majority of her family throughout her childhood and teenage years. Even her siblings bullied and beat her. Only her Aunt Baba and her grandfather Ye Ye gave her love and encouragement.

Falling Leaves is a courageous and unfaltering account of how she survived that rejection and, despite being humiliated and belittled by her family in her adult life, went on to become a successful doctor in the United States. It is a poignant and enthralling story of a Chinese family, torn apart with hate and feuds, from the time of the foreign concessions in Shanghai to the rise of Communist China and the commercial boom of Hong Kong. Adeline struggled simply to survive and learned to rely only on her inner strength to help her achieve her goals: to come through the nightmare of her childhood and make something of herself one day.

The hardback of **Falling Leaves** was published by Michael Joseph earlier last year to great acclaim. Amy Tan has described it as: 'Riveting. A marvel of memory. Poignant proof of the human will to endure ...' and Adeline's story has been compared with Jung Chang's *'Wild Swans'*. Chang herself described it as: 'Charged with emotion ... A vivid portrait of the human capacity for meanness, malice - and love.' In addition, Adeline has already been approached by two American film producers interested in turning her story into a screenplay.

Adeline Yen Mah will be available for interview and is also willing to write an article about her experiences. If you would be interested in talking to her, doing a feature/review on the book or even taking extracts from *Falling Leaves*, please contact Lydia Drukarz at Midas Public Relations on: 020 7584 7474.

Case Study

Getting publicity for an annual project

As well as publicising individual authors and titles, Coman Getty also have responsibility for promoting book-related events such as the annual Man Booker Prize and World Book Day.

With regular events it can be difficult to get journalists' attention. Whilst a prize features different titles and authors each time, and there is always some associated drama (who was left out, who was the surprise choice, who is the favourite?), a regular event without a shortlist can be difficult to promote. The key issue is how to get press attention for an event that they have covered before; how do you overcome their resistance and persuade them that the story is still news? Each year, a new pitch is needed.

World Book Day 2004 was the tenth anniversary of the event, and Colman Getty held a staff brainstorming session to come up with a fresh idea. I asked her if this featured any particular rituals: in the film *How to lose a guy in ten days* the magazine staff all take their shoes off before such meetings. She would confess only to lots of chocolate being consumed.

The idea they came up with was to see if they could make a link between different occupations and the books they like to read, and to try to establish who read the most. This produced genuinely interesting information that was also fun, and attracted attention in the national press, as well as in trade publications. Dotti Irving again:

'The key to finding a good idea is one that we are keen to talk about ourselves; to our friends and families. If you want to rush home and say "Guess what we found out today", it's a pretty good bet that we are on to a winning theme. This was a great idea that grew out of us all talking together, and that we all enjoyed working on. It worked extremely well and we got lots of coverage.'

Thursday 4th March 2004
www.worldbookday.com

Strictly embargoed until 00.01 hours
Thursday 4th March 2004

Accountants balance the books

- **Accountants are the best read profession**
- **Vicars spend the least time reading for pleasure**
- **Tolkien and Jane Austen still dominate the Top Ten**

Accountants spend more time reading for pleasure than teachers, MPs, journalists, taxi drivers and vicars, a survey commissioned for World Book Day reveals today.

The World Book Day survey asked members of different professions – accountants, chefs, clergy, journalists, lawyers, politicians, secretaries, taxi drivers and teachers – how much time they had to read for pleasure every week and what they enjoyed reading.

Accountants lead the way. They spend an average of five and a quarter hours reading for pleasure every week. They read all types of fiction, their favourite authors are JRR Tolkien and Jane Austen, yet they are also the most voracious readers of humour titles. They read mainly in bed or while commuting to work.

By contrast and at the bottom of the league, the clergy spend only an average of two hours and forty minutes a week reading for pleasure. Contemporary fiction by Alexander McCall Smith, Alice Sebold and DBC Pierre tops their choice of current reading matter but they also show a strong preference for Mind, Body and Spirit titles. Their runaway favourite novel is Tolkien's *Lord of the Rings* (with one preferring *The Rector's Wife* by Joanna Trollope).

Commenting on the findings, Kieran Poynter, UK Chairman of PricewaterhouseCoopers LLP, says,

"This just goes to show that you shouldn't believe everything you read about the reputation of accountants. The job can be a serious one, but the people who do it are just like those in any other profession. They come from all walks of life and have a wide range of interests, including, it seems, humorous literature. Long may it continue!"

The Bishop of Oxford, the Rt Revd Richard Harries, comments,

"Clergy need to keep reading in order to do their job and to remain alert theologically. Most of them do. This might count as work but for many of them it is also a pleasure. Total relaxed reading, however, is rarer because of the busy-ness of the life!"

Just behind accountants are secretaries who spend an average of 4 hours 59 minutes reading every week. Forty three per cent read most often in bed; their favourite authors are Jane Austen, closely followed by Terry Pratchett. Their current reading matter includes a high proportion of thrillers, particularly by John Grisham and Ken Follett.

Politicians, who read for just under five hours a week (4 hours 58 minutes), read far more biographies (47%) and history books (50%), often by other MPs, than any other profession surveyed. Their current reading matter includes Betty Boothroyd's autobiography, *Don't Call Me Madam*, Roy Jenkins on *Asquith* and *Friends and Rivals* by Giles Radice as well as *Caligula* by Allan Massie and a healthy dose of crime novels by PD James and Patricia Cornwell. Most of their reading is done in bed and they entirely eschew Mind, Body and Spirit and Self-Help books.

Journalists come a close fourth, reading an average of 4 hours and 57 minutes for pleasure every week. They are the only profession for whom *Lord of the Rings* or *Pride and Prejudice* are not their favourite novels – they choose Marquez's *One Hundred Years of Solitude*.

Taxi drivers come fifth, managing an average of 4 hours 46 minutes a week. Not surprisingly, half of all taxi drivers' reading is done while waiting in their cabs. Like politicians, a high percentage of taxi drivers (33%) particularly enjoy biographies along with thrillers (24%) and true crime (12%). Taxi drivers read more self-help books than any other profession.

Lawyers, in sixth place, read the highest percentage of crime fiction (41%) in the 4 hours 33 minutes they have to read every week. They have no time for poetry, gardening or self-help books or, in common with the clergy, romance.

Teachers and chefs come joint seventh, spending an average of 4 hours 27 minutes a week, mainly in bed or on holiday. Teachers' strong preference as current reading is for contemporary fiction over the classics but their favourite author is Jane Austen. The chefs voted for JRR Tolkien as their favourite author; lawyers, teachers and chefs spend more time reading on the loo than any other.

The effect of the BBC's Big Read is evident. Fifteen of the twenty most popular tides in this survey featured in the Big Read Top 21. As in The Big Read, *Lord of the Rings*, *Pride and Prejudice* and *His Dark Materials* are the top three favourite books for these professions.

Finally, those in the book trade – publishers, booksellers and librarians – were also surveyed but excluded from the main findings. Publishers and booksellers read an average of 6 ¼ hours a week, ahead of librarians (5 ¾ hours). But they would, wouldn't they?

- ends -

The World Book Day Just the Job Survey

	Accoun-tants	Secre-taries	MPs	Journ-alists	Taxi drivers	Law-yers	Chefs	Tea-chers
Types of books most enjoyed (3 genres nominated)	%	%	%	%	%	%	%	%
Contemp fiction	44	33	28	74	0	70	14	54
Classic fiction	36	31	34	28	2	52	11	35
Crime fiction	35	37	34	26	14	41	23	32
Biography	19	25	47	40	24	26	38	24
History	21	18	50	23	17	22	16	18
Thrillers	25	22	13	9	24	11	33	16
Fantasy fiction	15	10	13	6	12	4	18	17
Humour	20	21	6	17	7	11	10	16
'Chick Lit'	11	12	9	15	0	7	3	12
Travel	14	10	22	13	2	15	5	11
Sci-fi	10	6	22	6	14	4	22	7
Romance	10	15	3	2	5	0	3	13
Cookery	4	4	0	0	2	11	16	7
Poetry	3	7	6	6	0	0	1	7
MBS	3	1	0	6	2	0	1	6
Horror stories	3	9	0	0	7	0	11	2
True adventure	4	3	3	4	7	0	7	2
Gardening	2	1	9	2	0	4	1	4
True crime	3	7	0	0	12	0	5	1
War/Westerns	3	1	6	2	2	0	4	2
Sport	3	1	3	0	5	4	1	2
Self-help	1	0	0	2	5	0	0	2
Business	3	0	3	2	0	0	0	0
Where people spend most time reading	Accoun-tants %	Secre-taries %	MPs %	Journa-lists %	Taxi-drivers %	Law-yers %	Chefs %	Tea-chers %
In bed	35	43	47	45	24	37	40	50
On holiday	16	13	28	17	12	37	22	28
Sitting room	15	19	16	15	10	11	15	14
Commuting	26	18	9	15	0	11	3	1
Work breaks	1	5	0	0	50	0	10	0
In the bath	3	1	0	0	2	0	1	3
On the loo	1	0	0	0	0	4	3	2
Other	3	1	0	8	2	0	6	2
Av hours spent reading per week.	5hr15	4hr59	4hr58	4hr57	4hr46	4hr33	4hr27	4hr27

Summary of this chapter

Publishers rely on publicity to promote books – firstly because they seldom have large marketing budgets for more conventional marketing campaigns, and secondly because reading/hearing about new authors is an excellent way to engage people who might go out and buy the book.

But with more publicists chasing the same opportunities, and ever more authors starting to do the same, competition to get noticed is fierce. The more the author cooperates, the more likely it is that they will achieve coverage. So think carefully about how much you want to say about yourself, and try to be creative; look at your career and writing as the publicist might. And if anyone does respond, move quickly. Journalists have short attention spans, and space to fill. If one author does not provide the goods, someone else will.

11

Setting up a website

If you are not in the habit of surfing the web, you may not realise the importance of having a site of your own. As an author, it's a very good idea to have one, simply because it allows you to provide a flavour of both you and your writing, to those who find it convenient to search for information in such a way.

There is no point in quoting statistics about how heavily used the Internet is, because they will be out of date before this chapter is finished (let alone the book printed). Just as significant as the numbers involved is the social change brought about; once you have bought a particular product (e.g. flights) online, you seldom go back to working through intermediaries. Even if you are alarmed by the potential threat of identity theft, and prefer not to purchase in this way, seeking information through the Internet is so much easier than making endless calls to a telephonic directory service; you simply do a 'Google' search and then head for the relevant home page. Self-evidently, if you have no presence on the web, you cannot be seen.

'I think even a basic website, with an email address attached, is the most useful thing any author can have. Your readers can see what else you have written; they can email and tell you what they think (and they do!). These are your faithful readers (some of whom have turned into friends over the years) – the ones prepared to fork out a lot of money for a hardback, because they can't wait for the paperback, and may even pay large amounts of postage on top of that to have it sent halfway across the world. The least you can do in return is make yourself accessible, enter into this more personal dialogue with them through the newsletter, open the door on your world a little.'

Trisha Ashley, www.geocities.com/trisha_ashley2002

Examples of how author websites get used

The British Prime Minister referred recently to the 'Google Generation', and googling is indeed becoming a common habit. Journalists use author websites all the time, to find more information on those they are planning to interview or feature; they are looking for additional details to what was provided by the publisher. In the middle of writing a feature they may consult an author's site to gain a bit more background. When I am preparing introductions for talks I am chairing, I no longer go to the publishing house for information – it can take ages to get through to the right person, and even then they can be inclined to be forgetful and seldom send what I need. I have often found that I know more about the author than the person answering the phone! Instead, I now go straight to an author's website, where I can pick up interesting information provided by the author themselves. For example, I was chairing an event at the Kingston Readers' Festival recently, and spotted that on her website, the novelist Wendy Perriam (www.wendyperriam.com) – who was expelled from school for heresy – gave both God and the Devil a capital letter. This made a good anecdote. Similarly, readers who want to understand more about the writer whose work they enjoy frequently consult the web for more information. The message is clear: if you don't have a website, you risk being overlooked.

In some areas of writing, having your own author website is essential, as it is seen as a key part of what the author brings to the publishing product. In other words, as well as writing the book, being part of its promotion is vital. Pauline Goodwin, Senior Publishing Director of business information publisher Kogan Page, described having an author website as 'essential; all our authors must have their own'.

How to prepare yourself for having a website of your own

Do your research

I suggest that you begin by reviewing lots of other websites. Think about them critically, rather than just using them. As you do so, try to identify what makes a website work well or fail, from a prospective customer's point of view.

- Can you read it easily? Is the typeface easy to navigate; is it of an appropriate size (too small or too big can both cause difficulties)? How about the measure over which type is set – is it too wide? This is a common failing, which makes the text hard on the eyes.
- Do you like the tone of voice?
- Do you like the colours and images? Reversed-out text on a black background can be particularly hard to read.
- Is it restful or jarring, and does this match the subject matter?
- Is there any animation, and if so does it enhance the experience or just annoy?
- Is it modern or dated in feel, and which is appropriate?
- How do the ordering mechanisms work?
- How long do you stay (techies refer to this as the level of site 'stickiness')?
- Are there any gimmicks that you think would appeal to your readers, too?

Once you have thought about these points, try to decide whether or not the content lives up to your expectations. For example, what information should a user be able to find on a site? If you were promoting a restaurant, you might expect to find an up-to-date menu, details of how to find it, and information on where the raw ingredients are sourced from. How does this relate to a site for a writer? What kind of information do your readers require?

'I don't update my site often enough, but at least it is there, the first point of contact. I don't think a writer needs a big all-dancing, all-singing site either – I've logged onto those and they have taken so long to download I've turned them off again. And I'm bored by the ones run like blogs, with diary entries telling you what they had for breakfast, and what their friends said about their new shoes ... People log on to find out a bit about an author, what else they have

written, what is new, and possibly how they can contact the author to tell them what they think.'
Trisha Ashley

Accept that setting up a website will involve work on your part

You will have to think about what kind of information you want to present, and how you wish to come across. You will also have to decide how much time you are prepared to devote to updating it.

If you are going to have a website, and you want to encourage people to come back to it, you must give them new information and new reasons to consult it. This means that the site will need updating. Make it part of your regular routine: readers will be able to distinguish between a tone that comes from genuinely sharing information and one that comes from someone who begrudges the time it takes.

If you want none of this, then a simple home page (the first page the viewer sees, having looked up your site), a reference to your most recent work (with samples available), and a route to Amazon to buy the titles are probably sufficient.

Be prepared to ask yourself some awkward questions

Authors often moan about their jackets, claiming that their publishers have represented them as a particular type of author, appealing to a particular market – and that somehow the point has been missed. But deciding how you want to be seen means *really* thinking about what kind of image you want to present, and confronting some home truths.

I touched on the vulgarity of marketing language in my opening chapter. Most authors feel profoundly uncomfortable when it comes to thinking about these things. The word 'brand' is relatively familiar, meaning trademark or key identifying characteristics. Marketers 'position' a brand to have maximum resonance with the intended market, and a product's 'positioning' is the emotional relationship between it and the potential user. It follows that there may be a compromise needed between how your readers see you and how you see yourself, and you will have to think carefully about how you want to come across. Consider the following comment by Hunter Davies, on the process of 'ghosting' autobiographies:

'You're not necessarily trying to get their real voice, but rather the voice that the public believes belongs to them. For instance, with Gazza, I had to make it jokey because that's Gazza's persona. But in fact when I did the book Gazza was much more serious because he'd sobered up. With Wayne (Rooney), we all know that he's only 20 years old and has had virtually no education, so I had to keep it relatively simple.'[1]

If this feels uncomfortable, here are a few questions that may help you get started:

- What kind of people like your books?
- If you were an animal, what sort would you be?
- What sort of daemon would you have (see the *His Dark Materials* trilogy by Philip Pullman)?
- If you were a car, what would kind would you be (model and colour)?
- Many advertising campaigns are based around words that are thought to appeal to the market: thus, boy racer type cars are described as sleek and powerful. What words would you associate with you or your work?
- What is your brand? If you can't answer that, think about what kind of brands you would wish to be associated with.

'There was a time, not so long ago, when all a writer needed was a garrett, a Biro and a rackety love life. Not now; a writer needs a brand.' Jan Dalley[2]

How much information to share

Be aware that the more personal stuff you put up on your site, the more journalists and enthusiasts (who can be equally intrusive) will find to ask you about. If you share too much, you may end up feeling uncomfortable. On the other hand, because information on a website is presented by you, it does give you the opportunity

1 From an article on ghosting in *Seven*, 3rd September 2006
2 *Financial Times*, 30th October 2004

to put your point of view as you want it recorded – which is why press releases and important information about controversial issues are often put out by commercial organisations; *they* get to control the wording.

What kind of information to include

You can have fun here, drafting the web equivalent of a lonely hearts ad: a few words say so much. It is the quirky things that will really jump out at your readers – and they may either alienate or attract. Confessing (as I do) that you really like anchovies or marmite will have no impact with some of your potential readers, but may provide a bond with those who agree with you. What you really want to offer is a list of interesting opinions, without being over-dogmatic or too controversial. The last thing you want to do is give people excuses to leave your site, because they probably won't come back. You could feature:

* Books you adore/have influenced you
* Books you have recently read
* Favourite (and the opposite) places you have been to
* Most hated motorway or junctions
* Favourite sandwich
* Most hated words
* Preferred buildings (the de la Warr pavilion in Bexhill on Sea for me).

Options for setting up a website

Having spent some time thinking about what you want your website to represent, and what you might think of saying, here is some guidance on how to acquire it. You have four basic options:

1 Your publisher or agent may do it for you
2 You can do the whole thing yourself

3 You write it, then someone else designs and uploads it

4 You get someone else to do the complete job.

Obviously the costs will increase as you progress through these options. Don't forget to add a value to your own time: the assembly of a website may take up a great deal of this, particularly if you are having to read complicated manuals and learn new skills (such as the layout and uploading of pages) – and of course this may divert you from your own writing. On the other hand, the process of thinking about who will read the website and whom it will may appeal to can be an objective exercise in self-analysis – helping you think about yourself, your writing, where you are going with both (which is particularly revealing if you sense that the two directions are not the same), and whether you are marketing yourself as effectively as possible.

The publisher or agent does it for you

Most agencies and publishing houses have a website that lists basic information on those whom they represent and publish. Depending on how significant you are to the house, this may be a short entry, or a dedicated and bespoke site that has staff allocated to it and sends out email alerts to the faithful. For example, www.jacquelinewilson.co.uk is really a subsection of www.kidsatrandomhouse.co.uk, her publishing house's general site.

The plus side of this system is that someone else is bearing the costs and time of putting the site together. However, you may get allocated fewer pages than you would like, and your page will probably have a standard format that makes it similar to those of other people. To set against this is the fact that it's much easier for other people to 'write you up' than to do it yourself. Writing panegyric about yourself, or your own books, can feel a very dubious practice.

You can do the whole thing yourself

Some how-to books are now available: *Small Business Websites That Work* by Sean McManus (Pearson) is excellent, and the yellow and black *Dummies* series is also helpful. There are also off-the-shelf packages in boxed sets to tell you what to do; look in your local bookshop or stationer. You have the option of downloading templates online at low cost (google 'designing a website' to see just how much is available), but this is probably not advisable for beginners:

> 'Templates are a shortcut for experienced designers. Adapting the templates and putting your content in can be harder than starting a website from scratch.'   Sean McManus[3]

The main drawback of doing the whole thing yourself is that most authors first think about a website in an 'Ohmygod' moment, as they realise that those they are about to share a platform with, or aspire to be like, or live next door to, already have one. And if you end up having to teach yourself how to write and produce a website, you will either divert valuable attention away from your writing – or else end up with a second career as a website designer.

Basic design tips for those doing it alone:

- Avoid using too many different typefaces or types of bullet point, however sweet they look. The results can look like a ransom note

- Background images make text hard to read, so never superimpose text on a picture

- Black or a dark-coloured text on a white background work best; reversed-out text (for example the use of white text on a blue background) is exceptionally tiring to read – and tired eyes stop reading

- Similarly tiring for the eyes are wide text measures (the text spreads across the whole of the screen) so you have to move your head to read it all

- Big pictures take a long time to load, and so the frustrated new user, whom you cannot necessarily assume has broadband, may give up and leave your site

---

3 Author of *Small Business Websites That Work* and the ebook *Journalism Careers – Your questions answered*. His websites are at www.sean.co.uk and www.journalismcareers.com.

You write it, then someone else designs and uploads it

If you decide to employ the services of others, asking someone else to lay out and upload what you have written will cost less than asking them to organise the whole thing. But whereas many authors have drafted a flyer or press release about their work, writing a website is different. You have to think in three dimensions: which headings will lead on into which bits of further information?

You need a list of headings under which to divide the information you decide to present; writers usually opt for those that cover their main areas of activity (e.g. what you have written, your background [life so far], plans for the future, arrangements for booking you as a speaker, other matters of interest, etc).

Getting someone else to design your text should mean that your words are laid out in a way that draws in the reader. Few writers would think of themselves as layout artists when it comes to books and leaflets, and the skill in laying out a website is just as important. (This is the position I was in, and the solution I adopted. Go to www.alisonbaverstock.com if you want to see the results.)

> 'My advice here may seem obvious: get the best designer you can afford. A good designer will get a feel for your work and find ways of expressing it visually (and it is a visual medium more than a literary one). Mine suggested a Cambridge theme to match my series of Cambridge mysteries, so Cambridge blue and outlines of Cambridge scenes – rows of bicycles and so on – are a feature.'
>
> Christine Poulson, www.christinepoulson.co.uk

How to find a website designer

Website shops are appearing on the high street, and these firms will take your information and lay it out for you. Art and design students often take modules in website design as part of their course and so can be persuaded to lay out sites for you at a lower initial cost – because they have less experience and their overheads are smaller – but you need to think about what will happen when the information needs updating: will you still be able to find them/will the costs have risen disproportionately? Whoever you use, even though you draft the text yourself, check it again carefully once it has been loaded onto pages. Sometimes the process of setting up pages means that parts of what you supplied are re-typed, and what is uploaded may not be the same.

The UK Society of Authors' website lists website designers and specialists recommended by other authors. To find it, access the general site (www.societyofauthors.org) and then search for 'website designer' on the 'Help, Advice and Information' page; the search results page will give you the link for this information. This is part of the general information site and is not restricted to members.

Who should update your site?

You should. If you rely on the person who put the site up, your costs will grow – not necessarily because you are being ripped off, but because locating specific details and changing them can occupy as much time as coming up with an overall design. In addition, if you rely on someone else to do the uploading it will not be done as quickly as you would like. Changing to web-based promotion means that your timeframe changes; you start to want everything done really fast. You need the person who loaded your website to give you precise instructions on how to make the changes (or read the manual, if you are working from an off-the-shelf package), and then you need to practise doing it. From personal experience, the most difficult part is getting around to starting; you really can learn to update a website in minutes.

> 'It's all too easy to set up your website and just leave it sitting there in cyberspace. If you want people to keep coming back and to attract the attention of search engines you have to keep it up to date and add new elements occasionally. Put a note in your diary to review your site once a month.'
> Christine Poulson

Case Study

How to be the perfect client:
David McClelland of David Creative[4]

'Most authors seem to arrive at the point where they feel they need a website in a real hurry: they have just found out that their friend, rival or arch-enemy has one, and they think, "Well I need one too, and quickly!".'

The most important thing for you to think about, before you commission a website, is what it is for and what you want people to do as a result of visiting it. Clients who come to me having thought about these things are streets ahead – and get what they want relatively quickly. It's very difficult for me to design a website if you haven't considered what you want to use it for, so think – is it to prompt sales, to make your readers feel they have a relationship with you, or to promote advertising revenue.

To prioritise the function of your website, consider in what context you would find yourself saying (instead of describing your new book in painstaking detail): 'Why not have a look at my website?' Then think about how your new acquaintance would approach the site, what they would expect to find, and what you would like them to take away from the experience.

Before you talk to a designer, make sure you have looked at as many other people's sites as you can – and have opinions about how and why they work. This will help the designer get a clearer idea of what you want.

For most, your website will be the first point of contact people will have with you and your writing. So it is important to project the right image. I would encourage clients to give me samples of printed material that they feel visually encapsulates them and their work. From these references I can create a website that reflects you and your work through colour, typography and layout.

---

4 David McClelland combines his web design and illustration skills in a variety of projects aimed at both the adult and children markets.
http://www.davidcreative.co.uk

The actual building of the site can be done relatively quickly – in two to three weeks (dependent on the size and complexity of the website). The thing that takes the time is deciding what it's for and how to say it. And if a committee is involved it can take ages! On occasion, if a client's writing skills are particularly poor, I can write the words, but I'd expect a writer to give good copy! I'm happy to advise on what they should provide – I'd say the most common mistake is giving too much information, as reading on the web is generally quite tiring on the eyes and people don't want to scroll down more than twice. Lots of subheadings and short, concise paragraphs are best.

You get someone else to do the complete job

You may conclude that having someone tackle a job you have been meaning to do for ages, and look at you with an external, objective eye, represents money well spent. So if you have a mass of information, and no clear idea of what should be most prominent or where to start, it may be helpful to bring someone in to talk about content, layout and about self-organisation. They will help you to load information at a standard time in the progression of a job, rather than leaving it all in an amorphous mass in your head or on your computer:

'I need an effective website to represent the garden design service I offer. There are two main problems in getting on with this. The first is lack of time, to properly sort through all my photos and work out what I need to say. The second is that I have a background in IT, and so I know I could do it myself, which makes me feel that I should do just that, rather than pay someone else to handle it for me.

Time is limited. I am self-employed and there is always a new client to look after. So I seem to just keep designing and gardening – which is my purpose, I know, but it gets frustrating mentioning a garden I made this year and then not having the plans and photos to illustrate it in my portfolio.

What I need to do is to sit down and make time to think about how I want to present myself and what I want readers to understand. I need to put together the many testimonials I have had, both written and verbal, and combine these with images of work I have done. People tend to say very similar things about both my ideas and my working practices ("you have really listened to us"; "you are imaginative and the solution you have thought up will really work for us"), and the vast majority of my work comes through personal recommendation, which is lovely.

But new clients would find it reassuring to be able to see examples of what else I have worked on, whenever they happen to be considering my work – and without having to contact me. I also need to work the website into my routine. I am methodical about taking and archiving photographs – before, during and after the creation of a garden – but I need to see the website as a stage in this, so that before finalising any project, and moving onto the next commission, I load some images and a few comments on how the work progressed onto my website.

Deep down, I really want to do my own website; I know I would enjoy putting it all together, so am holding off paying someone else for the moment – it will become critical when I find I have run out of work from other sources or really need the website for other reasons. Whilst it would annoy me to pay someone else to do it for me, in time I may just have to accept that until I schedule in time to complete it, I may have to "delegate" (which is something I often found difficult to do in an office situation, too!).

I can see that employing someone to interview me and extract the ideas, put them in a logical shape and then upload them, giving me a timed requirement to load the pictures to match, would be a good investment. I crossed a related rubicon recently when, whilst out designing other people's gardens, I employed someone else to cut my hedge. Whoever does it, that's how I must see it; as an aspect of my business that I need to sort out.'

Susan Rhodes, garden designer

Sean McManus again:

'Whatever option you eventually select for the creation of your website, be sure to check out how it looks on the web and from someone else's computer, and from several other browsers (including

Firefox, Opera and Safari, alongside the market leader Internet Explorer).

The skill in web design is to make something that works on a wide range of computer and browser types and adapts gracefully to what's available. Even if a user is using an ancient browser that is text-only and doesn't handle pictures, the site should be usable. Authors have a responsibility to ensure that their content is accessible to people using assistive devices too, such as Braille readers and screenreaders that read websites aloud. There might be a legal requirement (under the Disability Discrimination Act), and there's certainly a moral imperative.'

What it costs to set up a website

How long is a piece of string? Costs can vary markedly according to how much the supplier wants the work (in the early stage of their career, they may be very keen to build a portfolio of working examples) and how difficult they estimate the client will be to work with. Clients who don't explain what they are trying to achieve, keep changing their mind, and then don't expect to see the increased time reflected in an increased bill, are particularly hard work, and there are many authors who fall into this camp. In general, and in life, costs rise according to the size of business doing the commissioning; thus if IBM were to commission a new website it would automatically cost more than for an individual author (unless you were extremely famous and in a tearing hurry).

Sean McManus says:

'Designers will quote based on how much work you ask them to do. That will vary by the amount of content you want on the site, and the sophistication of what you're asking for. Interactive features like content management systems so you can update it, forums so your guests can chat to each other, or games will cost much more than a text and graphics site. But they will also add some zing to the site that transforms it from a virtual flyer into an online experience. Once they've worked out how much work is involved, designers will adjust the quote for how easy they think you'll be to work with.'

As regards the costs of operating a website, McManus calculates as follows[5]:

- Access to the Internet, through paying an Internet service provider (or ISP) about £12 per month or £25 if you want high-speed connection through broadband. Broadband is often available bundled with landline phone, mobile and TV services.
- A website host to make your website available over the Internet, costing about another £10 per month for a reasonable small-business-level service. ISPs and hosts are listed in the back of Internet magazines, including *.Net* magazine.
- Buying your own domain name will cost an average of about £1 a month. This usually looks like your name:

  e.g. alison baverstock.com.[6]

- Alternatively, you can set up your site using someone else's resources and hosting, for example through Google's Page Creator (http://www.googlepages.com). But beware: Google can terminate the relationship at any time – which is why it's important that people reach your site (wherever it's hosted) through your own domain name. If your host goes down, you still control the traffic coming in via your domain name.

How to accept payment

Having a website also offers authors the chance to sell their publications and services online. Sean McManus suggests[7] several ways to sell books and make money from your website. For example:

- You can join Amazon Associates and receive 5 per cent of the retail price of anything that anyone buys (including competitive books) after following a link from your site

5 Source: *Web's Wonderful*, *The Author*, Autumn 2006 © Sean McManus, www.sean.co.uk and www.journalismcareers.com
6 Author comment: When websites were first available, several publishers experimented with 'clever' names (e.g. Harper Collins' first site was called 'fireandwater' because that was that their logo looked like), but found that most customers expect to look under the firm's name. The new generation of sites now tend to have the company name – and hence are easier to identify through a Google search.
7 Source: *Web's Wonderful*

- You can sell directly by using Paypal to accept credit card payments securely. This currently costs 20p per transaction plus 3.4 per cent of the transaction value. Paypal will also enable you to build a free shopping cart into your website. By selling directly, you can keep the entire retail share (bear in mind though that you will have to negotiate a discount deal with your publishers, store stock in conditions that ensure it remains saleable, and then pack up parcels and take them to the post office).

- Alternatively, you can have books and merchandise printed on demand and shipped through www.cafepress.com. Again, this costs nothing to set up.

- Once your site has a reasonable level of traffic, you might want to consider hosting Google's Adsense adverts. Google will feed adverts to your site that match your content, and pay you a commission on the money that it makes for any ads that are clicked on.

How to encourage people to use your site

Most people visit websites for one of two reasons: they want information, or they want entertainment. You can draw people in, and back, by:

- Ensuring that your site is easy to navigate. Jarring colours, too many images, and too many words all distract from the pleasure of viewing a site. Remember that most people browsing the web are looking for a pleasant experience; it's not compulsory reading.

- Using the right kind of words – *key words* that will drive people to your site (without overdoing it, because then search engines will think you are trying to trick them by manipulating your ranking, and you risk being banned).

  Use relevant key words and descriptions in the meta tags, titles and text of each page. Headings in the copy are picked up by search engines as being more important than the body text, so if the right words are used here, they will help the search engine find your website when someone enters keywords relevant to you and your work, and your eventual ranking may be higher. (McManus points out that this is assuming that the site is well designed and uses 'structural markup' – just making the headlines appear in bigger text has no impact on search engines.)

If your particular key words are already in use by someone else, it may even pay you to change your name. As romantic fiction author Catherine Jones commented:

'Anyone googling Catherine Jones finds several thousand matches – most of which are for Catherine Zeta Jones. Good luck to her for being so prominent, but tough on me, firmly in her shadow on the web. Now that I have decided to revert to my maiden name of Lace for my writing I expect people googling to find me rather than anyone else. Also, in the past, my books have only been published in hardback. I am not generally defeatist but I had to acknowledge that, realistically, there are few people who will spend £18.99 on a book when they can pick up something similar for £5.99. It seemed pretty pointless to try and increase sales through a website when I was hamstrung by the price of the product. Now I have got a contract with Little Black Dress who market their books at £3.99 ... Well, it's a completely different scenario and I plan to make the best possible use of the web to get the Kate Lace and Little Black Dress brands out there.'

- Use your email signature (the block of copy your word-processing package can add automatically to the end of all your emails) to advertise your website and your latest book. For example:

  Linda Strachan
  Author of *Hamish the Haggis* series, and many other books for children www.lindastrachan.com

Sean McManus additionally suggests[8]:

- Creating an email newsletter (free via www.yahoogroups.com)
- Offering downloads as a souvenir of a person's visit

8 Source: *Web's Wonderful*

- Asking visitors to bookmark your site and updating it regularly so there is something to come back for
- Offering free chapters or extracts
- Making signed copies available
- Offering additional material, such as chapters you deleted or characters you changed whilst writing – all to enhance the reader's understanding of the book you finally published
- Hosting a community forum where members can chat with each other.

'On my site readers can also sign up for a newsletter. I started a newsletter on my site earlier this year and it has been great fun – off it goes every three months or so, and back come lots of lovely emails from all corners of the globe. I have a prize draw every time for a copy of one of my books, and I've also been offering news-letter subscribers the chance to read a bit of my unpublished work.'

Trisha Ashley

David McClelland points out that, unfortunately, there is no magic bullet to get you straight to the top of a search engine result – but there are a few things you can do to ensure that people find your website.

- Publicise your website by talking to people about it, and include the website address on all your documentation (e.g. emails, letterheads, etc.).
- Create links (in both directions) to other websites that you share a common ground with (e.g. your publisher, other authors and online bookstores).
- Keep people informed of what you are doing by offering a 'sign up to receive my regular information bulletins' form. This creates a database of people interested in your work and ensures your future e-marketing messages will go to the right people.
- Allow visitors to tell other people about your website by including a 'tell a friend' button, which will email a link to and an extract from the page to the friend's email.

'Give the visitor to your site something to do with interactive elements. I've got a literary quiz and am planning a map which the visitor can click on for pictures of places that feature in the novels.'

Christine Poulson, www.christinepoulson.co.uk

Should you write a blog?

A *blog* is a type of website; a different way of managing website content. It usually functions as an Internet journal ('blog' is short for 'weblog'). In its most basic form, the software you use makes it easy to organise and publish written material – it works like an online diary that can be enhanced with video, photos, links to other sites, and even advertising. No real technical expertise is needed: if you have a computer and access to the Internet, you can sign up to Blogger.com or Typepad at either low or no cost, and have your blog established within a couple of hours. But you don't get paid for writing it, and it takes time out of your writing time, so why would any writer bother to produce one?

Why write one?

- It gives you a sense of who is reading you; most writers find this very motivating. Public Lending Right schemes that compensate authors for sales lost through loans by public libraries actually earn you little – but they still give you a wonderful sense of other people valuing your work, because they show how many people have borrowed your titles. In the same way a blog gives you a sense of others reading you – and it's more immediate, because you tend to get feedback

- It creates readers for your other works, because you can talk about what else you have published

- It fuels interest in you as a writer; in what makes you tick (and you don't need to be living a James Bond style action-packed life for readers to find this interesting):

'Readers like to know about authors' lives. Blogging is the perfect way of confiding in readers and strengthening the bonds of loyalty.'

Shoo Rayner www.shoo-rayner.co.uk[9]

9 *Read all about it*, article in *The Author*, October 2006

'If you decide to start a blog, it's best to have a particular focus. I decided to write about my life as a reader, figuring that people who like the books I write will probably also like the kind of books I read. Of course it all takes time, and all too often it feels like time taken away from writing the books that were the reason for the website in the first place. But I think it is worth it. Your website is a world-wide calling card.' Christine Poulson, www.christinepoulson.co.uk

- Not all those who read blogs are leisure readers; some are authors and agents – so a blog is a very public way of advertising your effective communication skills. Those who blog effectively report calls from speakers' agencies and TV producers, and all this on an international basis, at times when it's convenient for them to get in touch (and could not ring you)

- It gives you freedom; you can say what you like (there is no 'editing' or advice from the publishing house on what is appropriate). But whilst it's a fast format, the law is the same.

Legal considerations when writing blogs

Nicola Solomon[10], an expert in the law relating to publishing, comments as follows:

'Be aware that the Internet is not a law-free zone, so you should be as careful about the following points as you would if your work was going to be published traditionally.

Defamation. You have freedom as to what to write in a blog, but not if it is defamatory of another living person. Therefore ensure that what you say is true, accurate and can be backed up by facts.

Check that your blog does not include anyone else's work. Ensure that you have copyright clearance for use of any photos or illustrations. It is easy to cut and paste images from Google, but even if there are no copyright notices on them, re-use will normally be an infringement of copyright for which you could be sued.

Be careful when using photographs of others. If you took the photos then you will own the copyright, but the law of privacy may mean that you are not able to publish them on the web without the subject's consent.

---

10   Head of Intellectual Property at Finers Stephens Innocent LLP, www.fsilaw.com

Make sure your work is accurate; if following your advice could be risky, include an appropriate disclaimer: you don't want to be sued if your recipe for your favourite dish causes an outbreak of food poisoning.

Think about what use others can make of your work. Would you be upset if they re-used it? If so, include appropriate copyright notices and terms of use. If you don't know how to draft these, consider using a creative commons license

http://creativecommons.org/worldwide/uk

with which you can keep your copyright but allow people to copy and distribute your work on conditions which you can choose from a simple checklist given on the website. For example, you could allow your work to be used only non-commercially and amended, so long as you are given a credit.'

Other benefits of a blog

- You can try out ideas for stories and features that might turn into longer pieces
- In debate, a blog allows you to air your point of view without being interrupted, and then take comments
- It's a useful resource when demonstrating the craft of writing:

'After a while, I discovered that my blog was developing into an amazing resource for school visits. When asked if I have a special place where I write, I can turn to the interactive whiteboard – something that almost every class in the country now has – and show my studio and its construction to the children. Frequently, during a school talk, I wander off at tangents, explaining my latest passion or discovery. I might talk about the pond I built to be viewed from the studio, and how interesting it is to watch the wildlife finding the pond, using it and slowly populating it. Now I can show them what I'm doing as well as talk about it. There's a photo of the first living creature in the pond – a rat-tailed maggot. They love it. I photograph all the different birds that drink and bathe in the pond. I wouldn't bother if it were not for the blog.'

Shoo Rayner[11], www.shoo-rayner.co.uk

11 ibid

How long should you write for and how often? Some post every day; others at regular intervals, e.g. monthly. The only limitation on how long a blog should be is how much you want to write, and others want to read. Ultimately we write to be noticed and to communicate:

'I'm about to post my 42nd blog. They average between 1,000 and 2,000 words. I suppose I am helping to clutter up the great universal mess of words floating around in cyberspace, though I do take refuge in my quaint, old-fashioned belief that my blogs are better than most and worth reading. It's a belief that, surely, sustains all of us who write – or even blog.'

Tim Heald[12], www.timheald.com

Case Studies

How to incorporate web marketing into the promotion of your writing

Julie Cohen writes contemporary women's fiction, for two lines with two different publishers; in both cases it is the *line* that is marketed more than the individual title or author.

'I think being active online is the single most useful idea or initiative I have taken in getting me and my books better known and more widely bought.

I've been active on the eHarlequin website for several years, as a member of their community. At first, this was a way to learn more about writing romance and the publisher's requirements, but now that I am published by them, every post I make is, directly or indirectly, an advertisement for me and my books. I get quite a few referrals to my own website because of the eHarlequin forums, and have met several people who never post, but know me and have bought my books because of what I post (and I post at least once a day, and often quite a bit more).

12 ibid

This wasn't an intentional goal when I joined the community, but it's just happened to turn out that way. Except for forums such as expert Q&As that the website managers set up, I don't usually overtly promote my books on the site, though I do have my titles and website on my signature line. I just try to keep a consistently professional, upbeat attitude in my online posts, recognising that they're representing not only me, but also my writing career.

This takes up a lot of time, but I find it's useful for other things than self-promotion: personal support, finding out information, learning about readers, meeting friends and critique partners – so in all it's a worthwhile investment.

My weblog (blog), www.julie-cohen.com/blog, gets about 90 unique visitors a day (a unique vistor statistic only counts when a visitor clicks on your site for the first time). About 40 of those are regular readers, about 20 of them comment regularly on my site, and 50 are first-time visitors. As my first books only came out this year, I think these are pretty good statistics, and my return and first-time visitor count has risen steadily.

In addition, because I blog regularly, I have been invited to take part occasionally in group blogs (for example, www.romancingtheblog.com) which widen my readership; I've also been picked up on syndicated blog round-up forums. I exchange links with other authors to drive traffic between our blogs.

Blogging takes time, especially since you find yourself reading other people's blogs, too. I try to post at least every other day – sometimes about writing, sometimes about reading, sometimes about something in my life. Sometimes I use it as a warm-up to writing, and sometimes (I'll admit) I do it instead of writing. Most usefully, I blog when I'm mid-writing, when I have a problem or a breakthrough I need to talk about. I find it helps me to articulate what I'm doing, much like a telephone call to my critique partner. I also use it as an incentive, posting my day's progress every day I write.

It can definitely be a procrastination tool, though, so when I'm under deadline I try (often unsuccessfully) to limit my time in blogland.'

Chris Cleave writes contemporary fiction; his last novel *Incendiary* won the 2006 Somerset Maugham Award. He is currently writing a novel about an asylum-seeker in London, and is publishing his research in real-time on his website.

'Writing is vain without readers, so I enjoy hearing what they have to say and I try to write back. It makes me a better writer if I am sensitive to what readers were moved by in my work, and what they found annoying or superfluous. I've found that my readers are honest, interesting, and motivated to provide a kind of criticism that I find directly useful. Readers of novels, after all, are smart, independent and unconventional.

This direct link with readers would not be possible without the Internet. By maintaining a simple website I stay closer to my readers than if the communication was mediated by my publisher. My website (www.chriscleave.com) contains extracts from past work, "director's cuts" for fans, research for my current project and – most importantly – my email address. To me it seems the minimum of politeness, having expected the reader to listen to 100,000 of my words, that I should give them the opportunity to reply.

I think there is also some commercial sense in this approach. My publisher markets novels – they don't market the writer in between novels. That's the writer's own responsibility, and it's an important part of the job. I spend two hours a night replying to emails and updating my website, after the kids are in bed. My belief is that you win readers one at a time. They've made the effort to write to you, and if you make the effort to write back then it's a positive experience for both parties. Often the reader will tell their friends to read your book too. Sometimes they will review your book on their own website, or suggest it to their book club. Multiply that effect by 30 contacts a night, and suddenly you can pay for your kids' shoes.

Having a useful website is easier and less expensive than many people imagine. You need a normal connection to the Internet, ideally broadband. Then, using off-the-shelf free blogging software such as Blogger or TypePad, you can have your website up, running, and hosted for free, all inside of an hour. You just put your words into the templates provided. A good article at http://tinyurl.com/cvaof will explain your options. You don't need an expert to design or maintain your site for you. What you do need is the commitment to keep your site current and make it an interesting visit. Remember, you're a writer – visitors to your site are there for your unique point of view, not for your site's cutting-edge visuals.

Finally, do take the website seriously but don't let it screw with the part of your brain that writes books. Good luck.'

Summary of this chapter

Even if you never use the web yourself, you cannot ignore the fact that it's a hugely growing phenomenon, and those who find it useful to search for information in this way will not find information on you or your books if you do not have a presence there.

But before you go any further towards the creation of a website, understand that an effective site will have an impact on your working life, because either you or someone nominated by you must think carefully about how much time and effort you want to put into understanding how readers are using your site, responding to their needs, and keeping it up to date. The more thought you have put into these matters, the easier your designer will find it to work with you, and the lower both your set-up and maintenance costs are likely to be.

12

Working with booksellers, Amazon and other book retailers

The trade

When publishers and agents talk about 'the trade', they mean retailers whose main business is in selling books. When they talk about getting 'trade support' they mean persuading booksellers to stock their titles, and in sufficient quantities to make an impression on customers and hence prompt sales. 'It's unlikely to get much trade support' is an oft-quoted reason for rejecting submissions by authors.

It is worth pointing out that the balance of power between publishers and booksellers has changed dramatically in recent years. Publishers used to offer booksellers their wares to stock, and 'offered terms' (i.e. stated the discount at which they would sell) to bookshops. Now, the large chain booksellers increasingly dominate the market; they demand discounts in the confidence that if one publisher won't give them, another will. Significantly, many of this new breed of retailer are just that: retailers rather than booksellers, more interested in shifting 'product' (authors may wince, but that is how they see it) than the literary merits of what is stocked. The buyers in the largest chain booksellers also often shape the publishing programme today, and the view that a particular author or subject will or will not receive trade support can be a strong argument for the subsequent publishing decision. It's an irony that just as authors dwell on the misery of there being too many authors competing with each other to get published, so publishers constantly face a similar problem: there are too many publishers competing to get their wares stocked.

Extending the trade

There have always been department stores with book departments holding stock likely to appeal to their particular customer demographic (e.g. Harrods, Bloomingdales, David Jones). Now, though, a far wider range of organisations stocks books too. They have found that offering books for sale in non-book environments gives customers a wider range of things to purchase; what they want to achieve is total customer satisfaction, so that there is no need for people to have to move to another shop to find what they want.

New purchasing opportunities for the retail sale of books include the following:

- In supermarkets, the book zone can make a valuable browsing place for husbands and partners who would rather not be out shopping at all, and many books get bought as a direct result

- Similarly, those doing the weekly shop in a supermarket (and it is still mostly women) may slip a paperback by their favourite writer into their trolley and disguise within the 'domestic spend' a product that is just for them – in the same way that garages offer the chance to buy DVDs and gadgets. I know, I have done it myself

- When out at heritage sites at the weekends, books do well in the site shop, as many visitors like to bring back a keepsake

- Books can enhance the pleasure of purchasing other items. So, for example, offering books on whisky for sale in a specialist off-licence that stocks fine whiskies is an ideal way to create a sale. The customer – not unnaturally, given that they were entering an off-licence – probably had no thought of buying a book on the subject until the option was presented, then had only one choice (easy, and satisfying if a discount was incorporated)

- Farmers markets are now appearing in more and more places, and provided you can prove you are a local product, writers can sell their wares there too. Novelists Katie Fforde and Sue Limb enterprisingly sold their products at one, and found that they formed a valuable diversion from the other types of stall on offer (mostly selling food). Of course, there were no other books being sold to detract would-be customers from buying theirs. Selling in an otherwise book-free environment can be a tremendous opportunity.

The truth is that books can be sold pretty much anywhere people find it convenient to buy them, providing the housing mechanisms (how to store, wrap and account for them) can be handled. There is much that the individual author can do to help in such areas, to promote the profile and sale of their books.

Working with bookshops

I had a seminal experience as a student, when I saw someone being asked to leave a bookshop because they were copying down a recipe out of a title on sale. The manageress made the point that bookshops are not libraries; they are there to sell titles, not to offer information for nothing. And whereas most of the staff working on the shop floor are working in a bookshop because they find both product and atmosphere congenial, you should never confuse that with the need to be commercial.

When it comes to selling titles to bookshops, the bookseller is much less interested in what is in the book than who it will sell to and how great the demand is, so don't worry if information prepared for selling through shops is brief on content, and high on your sales potential. The rep selling titles (or 'subbing', which is short for 'gaining subscription orders') to a bookshop buyer or manager will also have precious little time to present each title, so it is crucial that the sales information presents the key details in a succinct and enjoyable manner – the key details being:

- Who is this author, and why have we heard of them?
- How well did their last book do?
- What will the demand be like for this one (any notable successes since last time, e.g. prizes won, news coverage achieved)?
- What is the publisher doing to support the title (advertising arranged, author tour planned, merchandising planned)?

For big titles (i.e. lots of sales expected), the publisher will prepare glossy sales brochures (often called presenters) which will draw a 'wow' factor from the bookseller.

Persuading booksellers to stock your title: the chains

Large stores with central buying patterns require presentations by publishers to their head offices, with all supporting information (author picture, planned book jacket, outline marketing plan) taken along. They do not see everyone who asks to go and talk to them, and will be primarily interested in the proof of demand for their products, and the associated mechanics of supply (how efficient, how much stock held, available how quickly?) from any potential new supplier. Thus the individual author who is trying to widen their stocking would be most unlikely to be involved with large chain order presentations (unless they were taken along as a 'prop').

There is scope however for author involvement in boosting stocking levels in their local branch of a chain bookshop. Even when such organisations order and distribute centrally, the shop managers of individual branches usually still have some discretionary funds for local purchase, and may be influenced to buy stock in support of local authors. But the buying process will be the same, and if an author is to persuade them that they should stock their title, they will need to be clear on (and unsqueamish about promoting) all the above points.

Case Study

Working with the trade

The Kingston Readers' Festival has been going for just five years. Right at the start we identified the need for book trade partners, and we approached Borders, who had recently opened a flagship store in the market square. It turned out that our approach was timely – they were getting increasingly concerned about the local shopping centre and customers' tendency to stay within it rather than venture out into other local shops.

In return for sponsorship of the festival, Borders agreed to:

- Host certain events; they have a large store which can accommodate up to 100 people in a pleasant environment
- Stock titles for all KRF events, including those from small independent publishers (we felt this had been truly born out when their poster for the 2006 festival featured a title by Welsh Women's Press Honno[1])
- Sell tickets.

Having begun with us, they remain partners in the enterprise. They have found that selling tickets and running events brings many new customers into the store, with special offers being coordinated to encourage them to buy whilst they are there.

Persuading independent bookshops to stock your titles

Independent bookstores have a very different ethic. With no central funding or expansive marketing budget available, all titles have to make their own way. On the other hand, they are free from centralised buying programmes – it's the experience of the owner or managers you have to contend with. Most independent bookshops are managed and owned by people who are passionate about reading and so tend to have strong tastes and opinions. If they decide not to stock your title, you may conclude that they are blinkered; if you get a positive response, you may consider them wise. But however you view them, it is *their* money they are spending – and risking – and that demands respect. Authors do not have the right to be stocked, just because they ask; the ruder they are, the poorer the response may be.

Approaching a small bookshop requires all the same preparation and relevant information as approaching the chains, but a particularly strong argument will be the local demand for your title. They will be particularly interested to know what you are doing to support publication through publicity, local events, etc.

1 *Losing Timo* by Linda Baxter

Also bear in mind that you are much more likely to get a positive response if they recognise you as a regular customer. You can't expect your local bookshop to be thrilled to stock your book if you have not put anything into the relationship first. The fact that you are local is not enough.

Case Studies

Helena Caletta of The Open Book, independent bookshop in Richmond upon Thames

I have been running this bookshop for 21 years – before that it was the Penguin Bookshop, and before that Pete Townsend managed a bookshop here.

This area is rich with authors, who often pop in. The shop is tiny but packed with stock, and I do try to take books by local authors. Partly this is because they are local – they are passing, so often tend to drop in to find out how their book is doing. But I also love to see enthusiasm in action. Reps come in and sell the next season's titles, but it's only occasionally that they say they have read something themselves or give you a proof copy. For the most part, they tend to present everything with a degree of uniformity and nothing jumps out at you. When an author is telling us about their own book, however, that can be really special. For example, I remember John Harding, who is a local journalist, coming in to tell me that his book had been accepted. We followed the whole process with him, from first copies, through reprinting, to television version, and TV cover tie in. We shared his joy in the whole thing, and that was lovely.

As the shop is long and thin, we have difficulty unpacking parcels and often have to do it by the front door. Last week I had 18 boxes, two days running! Authors often underestimate how many books we take. They are of course interested in their own book alone, but I really can't keep everything 'by the till' as so many request.

I also get involved in book events locally. I encourage authors to sign copies, as many of our customers like to buy them – it makes an ordinary purchase a little more special. There are ladies' lunches at which I sell books, and the Richmond Book Festival at which I lay on displays to support the programme. I try to be imaginative, and think about what else readers might like to choose, but a huge amount depends on how the author presents their talk. If they read their talk, rather than talk to the audience, or are condescending or sneer at the questions people ask (all of which I have experienced), we sell very few books. The irony is that they then go away cross – little realising that it was their performance that put people off, whereas we have mounted the display, and sold almost nothing, but our feelings tend not to be considered!

I am always pleased to hear from local authors who have a book coming out, but given that we have been here so long, we *really do* know the market. And as it's our money we are investing, please respect the fact that science fiction (or experimental fiction, if that's what you prefer to call it) does not do particularly well here, and so we don't stock it.

Tony West, manager of the Lion and Unicorn
independent and specialist children's bookshop,
Richmond upon Thames[2]

We are an independent specialist children's bookshop that has been trading in Richmond for 30 years. The many authors we have had in to speak to schools or for signings in the shop have tended to be arranged through the publishers, though local names will tend to drop in to sign stock when it is convenient for them. From time to time other authors or their friends will come in with books that have been self-published, finished and bound, and whilst I like to be encouraging I do feel that they misunderstand the way in which we like to trade. Whilst we love what we do, we are still a business and

2 Winner, Independent Bookshop of the Year (British Book Awards, 2000)

we cannot stock every title on the nod and a wink from a child reviewer or the well-meaning recommendation of a friend. Neither am I willing to flood our shelves with unknown titles in the run-up to Christmas, knowing how it will add up in the New Year if they haven't sold. Our customers do expect us to know our stock, and reading the new titles and proofs that come from the publishers we regularly deal with keeps us busy enough.

If the book looks like it has been typeset in the 70s, boardroom-style, or has been illustrated without an understanding of anatomy, I would advise a writer to start again with an editor or an agent, as children just will not pick up a book that looks out of date or unappealing. Many self-published books do not heed basic principles of good book design and I am not willing to take a chance on stocking a title that I believe our customers would not like to pick up.

Those authors who do want small bookshops to have access to their books would do well to submit titles to the wholesalers – Gardners, Bertrams or THE, who can distribute a book nationally if they stock it and with whom regular book trade terms and conditions apply.

It is a tough, competitive market out there, but if you have a good story to tell then it deserves a well-edited, well-produced package and writers should persevere with going through the recognised channels. There are plenty of people in the editorial divisions of the many publishing houses who should spot the potential of your story.

Persuading other kinds of large/chain retail outlet to stock your titles

Again, a head office presentation will be required. Supermarkets only take a very limited range of stock, and in very large quantities; it is most unlikely that an individual author could influence their central buying policy on their own. On the other hand, if you have a book of strong local appeal, and are offering a positive PR opportunity to your local supermarket (media coverage, charity appeal with a empathetic cause), a letter to the manager running the store, by name (ring and find out – and ask how to spell it!) with a suggested outline of how you might work together, could well result in a decision to stock your books.

Organising events in bookshops

It is increasingly common for bookshops to lay on events for their customers, and these offer valuable promotional opportunities for authors. Sometimes events are organised centrally through the publishing house, but many bookshops are willing to accept approaches from individual authors. Even very small bookshops may like to offer their customers 'signed copies', and this creates an opportunity for increased sales.

Find out if the store has an Events Manager; write down their name and contact details and send in a summary of what you can offer. Better still, go in and see them, but make a proper appointment – not just 15 minutes before you have to do a school pick-up or when your car is about to run out of paid-for parking. You want to be in a good state of mind when you arrive, and to give a professional impression. The way you present yourself now is a good indicator of how you will present on the night.

Ask them about the following:

- Do they run a book group, and would they like to choose your book and get you to talk about it?

- Do they run a creative writing group, and would they like a published writer to contribute? The audience can be just as fascinated by the process of writing (pen/pencil; late night/early morning) and how you manage to stick at it long enough to get published, as by what you have written. Having stock there, signed by the person who spoke, is a tangible record of the time you shared together, and hard to resist (so bookshops like it).

- Do they offer an open mike session for new writers to do readings?

- Would they like you to give a reading?

- Do they run a festival? Several now organise children's reading festivals.

What they will be looking for from you? Proof that your book is:

* new
* topical
* has a wide and identifiable readership ...

... and that you are both personable and good at talking.

Case Study

Ottakar's – now Waterstones – in Putney, London

We are part of a chain but feel that our shop has a distinct identity – and author events are a key platform in our activities. We hold a couple every month, although we don't schedule any in December and January as Christmas takes up all our energies then.

We charge for attendance, usually just £3, as we find that people are more likely to keep a commitment to attend if money has changed hands. In fact we do not make a profit on such events – everyone gets a glass of wine, and by the time that and the accompanying nibbles have been paid for, as well as the cost of the extra security required to keep the shopping centre open, we just about break even.

Most of our events are offered to us by the publishers. They produce a list of who is available for six months at a time. We know the profile of our customers and can tell by looking down a list of events which ones will work well. We then have to bid for them, against other shops – and sometimes ones in the same chain. We have to say how many we think will attend, and if we fail to meet the target the publishers can cancel (and have cancelled) the event. We would try to persuade them not to do that, and turn it into a more intimate event, sited in a different part of the store, so that those who have expressed a clear intention to come are not disappointed.

We get the stock in well beforehand, and often sell when we are promoting the event – some people like to read the book before they come along to hear the author, so they can ask relevant questions.

Other events are organised to tie in with our manager Mark Jackson's special projects. He runs a writing support group for local writers, as well as a reading circle, and all the people who attend are keen on events.

We are happy when local authors get in touch to suggest a reading; in fact those can be some of the nicest events, as they bring along friends and family and the local feeling of our store is boosted. But if authors get in touch to offer a reading, they must understand that it's us who have to take an objective view both of likely turnout and of potential sales, and we hope they will understand if we conclude that it will not work. Of course authors who are being offered by their publishers are shielded from this very direct feedback.

The best thing about organising events is the part they play in boosting community relations. We get a very familiar group of people coming along; some come whoever is talking, they enjoy listening to an author and having a book signed – and sharing a glass of wine with friends. That's just great.

Chantel Sulaiman, Events Manager, Waterstones in Putney

Good behaviour on both sides

If your publisher sets up an event for you in a bookshop, or a local firm agrees to host one for you, don't expect to be paid for the event. They will be buying in additional stock, promoting the event (once they have put their name to it they want it to be a success too), and selling books both beforehand and on the night, for which they may have to stay open late.

Some manage this with great charm. I did a talk for Ottakar's in Putney and once I had finished, and the audience departed, as a thank-you they asked me to choose any book I liked from the store. My response was to remember something my husband had said he wanted, and the wonderful events manager Veruska replied, 'How about something *you* want, as you did the talk?' What a treat for an author; like being a child in a sweetshop.

Good behaviour by local authors
- Buy locally. You can't expect a local shop to be thrilled to stock your titles if you never buy from them yourself. Being 'local' works both ways!
- Thank them for their support
- Keep them informed of their progress
- Arrange for proof copies/a free copy to be sent to them on publication
- Get a quote from them, and credit their inclusion (if they have given help, most people like to be mentioned. I know I do).

Poor behaviour by local authors
Don't:
- Park outside the shop that has supported you by taking your stock, with prominently displayed boxes from Amazon!
- Rearrange the stock and put your title at the front
- Hide competing titles in awkward places where they will not be found
- Drop competing titles behind the shelving.

And even small shops *do know*, because they have video surveillance cameras. What is more, most independent shop managers know their stock so well that they can see what has been moved in an instant, in the same way that you might notice if someone has been into your house and changed the arrangement of your possessions. So they know what their customers are doing – even those who are not really customers, but have instead come in to see how their books are selling!

Working with Amazon

Amazon is a convenient way of ordering books, and their suggestions – prompted by what you have bought before – can be very helpful in directing you to new titles.

Amazon offers all site visitors the chance to review titles. There was a heated debate in *The Author* magazine a couple of years ago, when one author pointed out that it was easy to encourage your friends and relations to respond to the site request to 'review this title' with positive reviews and five stars; a flood of correspondence followed in the next issue about this cynical manipulation of the medium. Having mentioned how to do it, I leave this to your conscience.

> 'I was happy to receive a free copy of my friend's book, and enjoyed reading what she had written – it was quite an insight seeing inside her head, to be honest. A few months later she rang to ask if I had liked it, and when I said yes, if I would be willing to write a review on Amazon. I did not mind her asking at all, I was glad to be helpful, but I do wonder when I will get around to it. I use the Internet very little at work (I am a lawyer), so plugging in my laptop and working out how to do this will take time – the one thing I have precious little of. It's funny how people who use the Internet a lot assume that everyone else does too, and she had to explain several times what was required. But I absolutely did not mind being asked, and as writing a book is something I could never do, I am happy to encourage others who can. And I will get around to it, especially as I have now told you.'
>
> Shirley Evans, solicitor

Amazon also offers the opportunity for you to comment, as the author, on why and how you wrote your book. These can be really interesting insights into the writing process.

Reading and writing websites

There are many other reading and writing websites and message boards on which authors can post interesting things and spark debate. Several publishers offer chat rooms associated with their key authors' pages, and these all boost reading and discussion. One of my favourite such sites is www.meettheauthor.co.uk; this is a fascinating site, with authors giving unscripted short talks about their books, and what inspired them. Supported by book wholesalers Bertrams, and available through large chain stores and airport terminal bookshops (where the potential purchaser often has more time), I find the short videos make compulsive viewing.

Summary of this chapter

The book trade exists to stock, promote and sell books and other related items. If as an author you hope they will take your titles, you have a duty to promote these outlets, buy from them yourself, and promote the value of the book in general.

Whilst booksellers may love what they do, they are in business to make a profit, and authors should remember this. They will seldom stock books out of loyalty alone; they have to be convinced that they will sell.

13

Literary festivals, working with libraries, reading and writing circles, and other chances to talk about your book

A creative climate

Once upon a time, books were sold through bookshops and reading was a largely private pursuit. Over the last ten years, however, several important things have happened so that books are now available from all sorts of places, and can be backed in a variety of ways. What is more, amounts of government money are being used to persuade non-readers that books are something they might enjoy, too.

Trends in book stocking and buying

- An exponential increase in the number of books being published, so that it is arguably no longer possible for bookshops to stock a representative selection

- A huge increase in consumer confidence in buying products online, and the increasing sophistication and personalised feel of systems of recommendation – such as Amazon 'Readers who bought this title also chose ...'. Online *can* feel personal

- The end of resale price maintenance for books, which means that they are no longer definitively priced by the publisher, but can now be discounted. This has led to a range of stock being 'price-promoted', and a consequent reduction in the range held (lower profits are made on price-reduced stock, so booksellers compensate by stocking them in bulk)

- A change in the book trade, with much more severe decisions made about the desirability of stocking titles that have a low stock turn (i.e. the number of times an individual title is bought and sold – or the stock turned over – within a given period). Many chains have also moved to central buying, which means that the stock is ordered centrally and despatched to individual stores according to the local demographic. Local buying power has been reduced.

Trends in book enthusing

- Many other vehicles have emerged for enthusing about and selling books. There are now a number of festivals (both literary and those that have a section on books and reading), and there has been a huge rise in the number of reading circles meeting and discussing books; the majority are privately organised, but some are organised by libraries, arts venues and bookshops

- Media companies have discovered that books, authors and readers make interesting – and cheap – television. The BBC campaign to find Britain's best-loved book (*The Big Read*), and reading promotions on Oprah and Richard & Judy have had a huge impact on the number of titles bought – it was estimated recently that one in eight titles bought through a UK bookshop was influenced by Richard & Judy choices

- Other book initiatives: Chicago tried to get the whole of the city reading *To Kill A Mockingbird*, and this initiative – to encourage everyone to read the same book at the same time – has been copied on both sides of the Atlantic; in Bristol it spread out well beyond the city to include the whole region. Many US universities run programmes to get the entire new entry of freshmen all reading the same book before they arrive, and discussion groups are held during the first week of term as part of a programme of bonding and settling in

- Creative people in residence schemes have widened the under-standing of the benefits they bring to society, as have public roles like the Children's Laureate. Tracey Emin's appearance on the popular (but utterly middle-England) radio programme

Desert Island Disks convinced large swathes of people, who know instinctively that they do not like her art, that she works very hard and that creative people who think differently have a value.

There are lots of opportunities for authors to benefit from this newly creative climate. The remainder of this chapter is devoted to thinking about how the author can help their own profile, and that of their writing, through such schemes – thus making the most of the promotional opportunities available. Sometimes this will be done with the support of your publisher, and matters will be arranged by them; sometimes you will have to go it alone.

Festivals

Festivals of reading are growing, and it's not hard to understand why. Readers often build up a strong rapport with a writer whose work they enjoy, and with the characters they have read about, and want to hear first-hand how the books came into being. There is also an enduring fascination with how the author looks; many who have been touched by a particular book want to listen to the author speak. As well as those who appreciate the author's work, there will be others who want to know how they did it, perhaps to support their own writing ambitions. They will be fascinated by the details of the writing process: pen or computer; morning or evening; with or without whisky/music/the support of others. Less obviously, I think the growth of festivals also draws on the growing automation of everyday living. With so much that can be ordered online, without speaking to anyone, at any hour of the day or night, consumers are looking for a higher-grade interaction in other aspects of their lives – hence delicatessens, cleaning services and florists have never been busier. The chance to meet an author at first hand can be a real draw.

The British Arts Festivals Association (www.artsfestivals.co.uk) has a representative sample of the UK festivals sector amongst its 500 members ranging from the Edinburgh International Festival at the large scale down to smaller town and village festivals. Over the past decade some important changes have happened to the sector:

- Programming has diversified. Many of these festivals began as classical music events and now embrace a wide range of art forms, including books and reading

- Some of the larger events now run more than one festival, such as Cheltenham, which today boasts an international music festival, a jazz festival, a literature festival and a science festival. Other festivals, such as Brighton, also run venues throughout the year

- Many arts festivals in the UK run some sort of education programme alongside their festival; often this is work that happens throughout the year and culminates during the festival period

- Local authorities in the UK have seized upon the idea that festivals can be good for regenerating cities, and so, for example, in Manchester a new International Festival will be launched in 2007 which is designed to show Manchester as a forward-looking city.

Publishers now include literary festivals on the programme for author tours. Most festivals either have a sponsoring bookseller who attends with stock of the titles of speakers and related items, or one of their own (as in Edinburgh). Sometimes your publisher may suggest contacting festivals to arrange for you to speak; at other times you are better placed (or just better motivated) to contact your local festival and find out if there is an opportunity to get involved.

Programmes get planned a long time ahead, so information should be with them a minimum of nine months before the events scheduled. Remember:

- Don't just send a list of your books, emphasising the new one; try to format these into events that sound interesting. Most festivals organise themselves into various strands of entertainment (e.g. Edinburgh offers 'Fine Fiction', 'Lived Lives' [biography and memoir] and 'The Writing Business' [how to write and get published]). There are programmes devoted to new writing everywhere, but the organisers may also be looking for contributors to a panel-based discussion that, whilst book based, raises and discusses current issues

- Include relevant author information, and in particular your local connections

- Include proof that you are a good speaker – feedback from previous occasions, copies of cuttings from the local paper, mention of your website where you have links to recordings and interviews. This may mean that you take up events as practice sessions, maybe offering a talk in your local library or to a readers' circle to gain confidence

- Consider media connections, interviews on local radio; what else you can do to 'support the event'? How can you help ensure that there is an audience?

Sometimes you will get paid, sometimes not, and it is up to you to decide whether or not to accept the gig – perhaps with the wider aim of general publicity. Sometimes publishers will book you to attend a festival without considering whether or not a fee should be paid; their interest is in the book that they have invested their money in selling, not in the author earning. If this happens to you, try to sort it out with the publisher: the festival organiser is likely to take the view that it's something the author and publisher ought to be communicating about.

You may ask yourself why, as at most of these events people are paying to attend, a fee is not routinely offered to the author. The simple answer is that most festivals run on a shoestring, and arts funding in this country is limited.

'The problem for most festivals is that offering even a token fee to every author would add thousands to already stretched budgets. Without increases in subsidy across the board, that would inevitably mean increased ticket prices, which would hit audience numbers at events with new and unknown writers hard, and discourage even the most adventurous festival programmer from taking risks. On the plus side, festivals give authors a chance to sell their book; provide additional exposure in the regional and national press, often with the chance of local radio and television interviews; and spread your name far beyond the festival audience, as people pass the word to friends and neighbours. And appearing at a well-known festival looks good on any writer's CV.

In addition to money from the Arts Council, many literature festivals are also funded by their local authorities (Ilkley is partly funded by Bradford Metropolitan Council); some are actually staffed by the local authority or run through library services – Bradford, Beverley and Sheffield to name but a few.

Arts funding is always limited and there would need to be a whole different level of funding if authors charged a fee for events as standard. It would be as if Equity negotiated a 50 per cent increase in fees for actors across the board and subsidy for all major theatres had to increase commensurately. Authors might need to start a national campaign, or persuade publishers to pay them for book tours as a standard clause in their contract.'

Rachel Feldberg, Director, Ilkley Literature Festival

It may seem to you unfair that the public are being charged for tickets, booksellers are flogging titles, and the fee you are offered is low or non-existent, but the realities of running such festivals are much harder-edged. Even if you cannot get paid, and must rely on expenses (it's very unusual not to offer these), you may find it is worth doing anyway, for exposure and raising your profile. The festival handling the event will be promoting you through its programme. Offer them a photograph. Most have an associated website that can feature your information and link to your own.

Library talks

Libraries used to be places where books were chosen by readers, and promotion of one title in preference to another was seen as invidious. How things have changed! Librarians are now actively trying to encourage wider use of their facilities, and there are librarians charged with the special role of reader development whose remit is to expand the reading taste of the local population by offering them interesting tempters. The audience for such talks comprise mostly the library users – often those at home with young children, the retired, or those with time during the day – but they may be particularly pleased to attend a relevant talk (although sometimes their enthusiasm, and knowledge, can prevent the speaker from getting enough time to deliver what they came to say). Audience control can be a problem when the listeners are packed with opinions too!

Most local library authorities have a Reader Development Officer, and Fiona Allison, who fulfils that role in Kingston upon Thames, commented:

'Reading is much more of a participatory activity today, partly due to the huge rise in book groups, and bringing authors and readers together is all part of my role in encouraging wider reading.

Although readers enjoy meeting and hearing their favourite (often better-known) authors talk about their books and how they write, it is equally important for libraries to support and promote new authors, who have yet to develop a readership base; the events I run try to reflect this.

I am contacted on a regular basis by new authors, usually by email, who are self-published or with smaller independent publishers who aren't able to support full promotional book tours, but who would like to have the opportunity to talk about their books to readers. I also sometimes become aware of new local authors through articles in the local newspaper, and I will then contact them offering the libraries as venues to do a talk and sell copies of their book.

The larger publishing houses may contact me directly when they are trying to organise a book tour for an author. We are unfortunately limited by our venue space in some of our libraries, and often publishers want a guaranteed audience number, which we cannot meet, so it is harder to attract the "bestselling" authors.

At all the events I organise, I arrange for books to be available for selling and signing, and I will often purchase additional copies for the libraries.

Two years ago, 'Reading Partners', a partnership consortium between public libraries and seven leading publishers, was established, offering direct access to authors, book events and the opportunity for authors and publishers to work with reading groups. I now receive specific contact details of authors and their publicists in advance of book launches/promotional tours and this makes it much easier to directly organise library events.

'Reading Partners' has been a huge success and has allowed more authors to reach readers through the public library network across the country.'

Case Study

How this works for the author: interview with Dr Jacqueline Banerjee

'I gave a talk in Surbiton Library on 'Literary Kingston' and was surprised and delighted to find an audience of about 100. Alison was there and asked me how the librarian found me. It's a long story.

I spent my career teaching English literature in universities all over the world, and settled back in Walton-on-Thames five years ago. Given my professional background, I became fascinated by the number of writers who had lived locally and began researching a book on the subject. *Literary Surrey* came out in 2005 from a small independent publisher, John Owen Smith (www.johnowensmith.co.uk). Whilst researching the book I bought several titles from our local bookshop and told them about the progress I was making; one of my sons was also a good customer of theirs. When the book came out, they suggested – and hosted – a lunchtime drinks party with two other local authors from 11.00 to 12.30 one Saturday. There was a steady trickle of visitors and it was very pleasant, but I did not think much more about it. I was surprised at what resulted.

They had arranged for the local press to take pictures, and this spread the word wider. The book began to sell well through the shop. As a result of someone's purchase, I got asked to give a talk to a local reading circle, and then to give several talks in the area; one of these was in Surbiton. The librarian who had booked me to talk had sent emails announcing it to her many contacts in the area, and put up posters in all the local libraries. As time goes on the audiences for talks seems to get bigger, and more books get sold.

As well as sending review copies to the local papers, I also approached several literary societies set up for writers whose work I cover in my book. Some were very proactive in promoting me. I took the book to many of the local museums, heritage sites and visitors' centres (and even to a pub which was particularly associated with one of the writers!) and asked if they would like to take some copies on a sale-or-return basis. Most were friendly immediately; all were eventually, once they realised it would sell (I never had any copies returned). It does particularly well through Denbies (a local vineyard and tourist attraction) and The Box Hill National Trust Visitors' Centre. Interestingly the shop at nearby Claremont Landscape Gardens (also NT) seems to do better with cookery books – the profile of visitors to each venue is quite different! I came to an arrangement with another local author that he would represent my book in bookshops he is visiting, and when I am talking he is welcome to come along and display his books as well; that helps him, too.

I didn't have to promote my previous books, which were published by bigger publishers, but I think promotion is essential if your book is of local interest and your publishing house is small. It's not something you have to keep doing – once shops and other outlets realise that it sells, they reorder quite easily, but you must get the thing started.   In the end, I really enjoyed the experience, and even made some new friends through it.

The one thing I would do differently if I was writing from scratch right now? I would have thought more carefully about which writers to include. People want to see their own localities in the index, so had I included more writers, in more parts of Surrey, I would have reached even more readers.'

Dr Jacqueline Banerjee, author of *Literary Surrey*

Reading circles

The explosion of reading circles throughout Britain offers interesting opportunities to authors, and many welcome a local author to come and talk about a book they have read. Apart from prompting eight or ten sales (the size of most such groups), and possible further stocking by local booksellers if they see that titles are selling well, the first-hand feedback on your writing from people who have really engaged with your work can be terrific. Ask around to find out where reading circles are running, or in your local library, which also often hosts one.

I received an email from an author I had met at a Society of Authors event, referring to the fact that I had mentioned I was part of a reading circle, and asking if I would consider choosing her book when it was next time for me to make a choice. Examining why I did just that may be interesting for those considering asking a similar question. I said yes, because:

* The question was not raised too soon into the relationship, but followed on from a series of backwards and forwards emails talking about matters of overlapping interest
* There was no chasing or checking mechanism to see if what she had suggested had been taken up
* And the suggestion was made so deftly.

Case Study

How it feels to attend: interview with Lakshmi Persaud, author of Raise the Lanterns High

'Talking to a book group or a book club is both pleasurable and challenging for me – whether I am offered an honorarium or a fee, or simply the delightful experience of meeting readers who read with care. Pleasurable in that it is always nice to be invited, and challenging in that you are about to face a number of points of view and interpretations of the novel. I approached Alison's group-reading of *Raise the Lanterns High* in this way.

I discovered the characters anew; whilst I thought I understood them already, I am receptive to what readers think, and so listened with care. With this group the conversation moved back and forth, with explanations of certain unspoken aspects of the culture that energised the thoughts and behaviour of my characters.

A highlight of the evening came when the readers, almost imperceptibly, could see that they as parents, in their own way, would also try to influence the choice of life partners by their offsprings, and that the educated middle-classes still have their preferred choices regarding behaviour and outlook. Whilst their method was different from that of the parents in *Raise the Lanterns High*, in that theirs was more in keeping with a society where parental control begins to be relaxed from an early age, the group was able to see that in essence, their values were similar. All wished for a similar "good life" experience for their children.

The discussion overflowed into the meeting of traditional cultures with the strong individualism of British culture; it was brought to a reluctant closure by the timetable of the trains.'

Talks in schools

Creative writing is part of the educational curriculum, and from their early years in school onwards, children have to study different forms of writing. It follows that hearing a talk from a writer can be an effective method of inspiring them, and writers are welcome in most schools.

Sometimes you will have to do the talk for nothing more than a thank you (although the school will probably buy some of your books out of courtesy), but there are other schemes to support visits. For example, in Scotland the Scottish Arts Council will pay for writers to do talks in schools; there is a standard fee of £100 per visit and writers sometimes take a few days off writing to tour, talk and earn some immediate funds in this way. And whilst the children will probably enjoy listening, the author gains first-hand feedback from the market, which can be invaluable.

Other opportunities exist around wider book promotional schemes such as National Book Week in the UK, World Book Day, and schemes linked with local festivals and prizes. Some local educational authorities will require you to have personal insurance whilst you are working on school premises. Your national or local authors' organisation should be able to advise, and may even recommend a specific policy to members, at a discount.

Case Study

Guidance on how to run an effective author event in schools

Children's author Nicola Morgan wrote the following for the *Times Educational Supplement* (Scotland):

'Books change lives. Author visits can, too. Good author visits turn non-readers into readers, readers into book-lovers. And bad author visits? Are there such things? Er, yes. Bad author visits leave authors mentally bruised, and pupils oblivious – the worst outcome. I'd rather fall on my face than have pupils not notice I'd been. In fact, the worst question I ever fielded after an hour-long event was, "Who are you?"

The best events are *not* always in the wealthiest, most book-oriented schools. They are in schools which have thought extremely carefully how to spend their money and made huge efforts to add value. Preparation is the key.

Choose and invite your author

Why *this* author? Time spent researching your author pays dividends. Ask other librarians/teachers for recommendations (but don't forget untried authors – they may be excellent speakers too).

Most authors have websites, often with advice about inviting them to speak. The relevant page on mine is called, unimaginatively, "Inviting Me To Speak". Authors are all different, with different skills and personalities; we offer and need different things; but we *all* want to provide great events.

Once you've identified your author, communication is essential. Be clear about your wishes but accept that the author knows what works for him/her. Agree times, audience size/age, and the exact nature of the event. Ask about technical requirements and mention any pupils with additional needs. Which books will the author talk about? Should pupils have read any? Some authors (including me) don't mind; others mind a lot. Is particular preparation by teacher/class useful/necessary? Will pupils need paper or pens at the event? What travel arrangements and costs are involved?

Money issues

Clarity about money is vital. The root of all evil is tangled, and there is frequent confusion about what a "session" is. For clarity: it is *one* talk/workshop. It will probably be, on average, an hour. A workshop is often longer, perhaps 1.5 hours, and may cost more. A session with younger children may be shorter. If your timetable only allows 40 minutes, then a session is 40 minutes. The point is: one session = one fee. A shorter session is not a smaller fee, as losing 10 minutes does not reduce preparation time or energy. Of course, compromises can be reached, and it's worth asking, explaining your parameters. Some authors have a minimum daily fee, because travelling can use a whole day for one event.

Selling books

Some authors do; others don't/can't. Some schools find it problematic and we do appreciate this. But owning books really encourages a love of reading. And, frankly, authors don't earn money if their books don't sell. (Violins away now, please.)

If you *will* be selling books, discuss the author's recommended structure, including supply of books, help with selling, pricing, float. And *please* encourage/remind pupils to bring money – very often, pupils are disappointed because they find they want to buy but forgot money.

Prepare pupils – and staff

Making the pupils excited really affects the event. It's possibly the most important thing you can do. Exaggerate our fame – we won't mind! Get them to use our websites and prepare questions. Ask our publishers for promotional material. And do, please, ensure good staff presence and decent behaviour from pupils. The author's energy should go into inspiration, not discipline.

On the day
After this preparation, the day will be a doddle. Only two things to remember now: 1) a glowing intro and thanks 2) tea/coffee. Add chocolate chip cookies, and your dream event is assured.

A well-prepared event, with an inspirational author and interested staff, can be mind-opening for pupils. Your own children's authors are an incredible resource, living on your doorstep, keen to do the best possible talks for you. Use us, with preparation, communication and enthusiasm. Together, let's turn pupils into booklovers; let's change lives.'

Writing circles

There are also opportunities to give talks to writing circles. These are variously organised, from the highly proactive, who publish anthologies of their members' work in anthology form (e.g. the Oxford Writers Group, www.oxfordwritersgroup.com), to groups who just meet in the pub for a chat at regular intervals. Most have a programme secretary who arranges speakers, and they are often keen on using local writers. The standard of engagement with your work can however vary enormously, from the intelligent interaction which gives you real insight, to the downright rude. You may often have to bite your lip:

'I have not read any of your books, but people tell me they are similar to JK Rowling's. So how come she is famous and you are not?'

> Question to Philip Pullman at a talk he gave to a local writing group, a month before he won the Whitbread prize

Who else might like to hear you?

There are lots of other organisations, not book-related, that meet at regular intervals in most centres of population: arts associations, local political clubs, The Round Table, language clubs, etc.; your local council should be able to provide some information to get you started. Ours includes on its website details of many organisations and societies that operate locally, with information on how to contact them. It is worth bearing in mind that the vitality of each organisation is a direct function of how lively those running it are, and this will obviously vary from region to region. You cannot assume that because the branch of a specific organisation in your own town is completely moribund, others will be too. In addition to looking at official lists of organisations, it is also worth finding out about the following:

- Which organisations do your friends and colleagues belong to, and which offer the kind of programme that is most naturally suited to accommodate you? Are there any organisations to which friends could put in a good word for you? Sometimes the names of such societies can give little impression of their level of vitality. Where I grew up, the most thriving association in the town was The Citizens Association, which sounded fearsomely dull to a teenager. But their programme of speakers, as I was forced to admit once I reached the Sixth Form, really was interesting. I even went along a couple of times

- Read the correspondence columns and advertisements for forthcoming events in the local paper to pick up ideas

- Look at the noticeboards in your local library and ask about related associations at the information desk. Leaflets on local societies are often available here, too

- What about educational institutions in the neighbourhood? Are there any well-known schools, a university, adult education college or further education college? Offer to speak at one such institution, and make a good job of it, and you may find your name passed on to others

- We've mentioned literary festivals, but find out if there are any others going on in your area and further afield (again, the library noticeboard is a good starting point). General town festivals and flower festivals often have accompanying programmes of talks from visiting speakers. And some festivals are linked with urban renewal, so local writers can be welcomed back. Writers are sensitive people, however, and if the birthplace in question shows no interest at all in their famous son/daughter, it may be held against them in the long term:

'There is a real dilemma in my home town about me. They are delighted that someone from Bandon is on the television; they just wish it didn't have to be me. Even my school has never once asked me back to do a single thing, not give a speech, cut a ribbon, turn a sod – nothing. Sadly, should the invitation come now, it's too late. I'll save them the expense of stamps by stating simply here: fuck off.'

Graham Norton, *So Me* (Hodder & Stoughton, best in CD version, with him reading it)

Summary of this chapter

The fact that you have published a book makes you interesting to many people, either because they are fascinated by your subject, or because they want to learn from your experience and spot how they could get published too. Provided you make a reasonable job of it (see advice in the next chapter), it can be a really important way of both widening your profile and promoting sales of your books.

14

How to be the perfect speaker

This chapter follows on from the previous two on opportunities for authors to talk about their books. Having described the options available, how do you make contact, get a booking and deliver what is expected?

I understand that there will be many authors who feel that arranging to give talks on their book is something that their publishing house should sort out – and if you are famous, or your book particularly newsworthy, they may do just that. On the other hand, for the mid-list author, who might feel that he or she is not at the top of their publisher's 'to do' list, arranging matters yourself is a good idea. Firstly it avoids the frustration of relying on someone else, and secondly you probably have a much stronger idea of local possibilities than your publishing house. What is more, the process of setting things up builds an impression of you as a proactive person; you widen the public's appreciation of yourself and your books, and you sell stock – all of which are likely to further cement the author-publisher relationship.

What you need to know

The previous chapters provide lots of ideas on what kind of organisations to contact. But before you write to them to offer your services, you need to find out the following – either from the organisation itself, or perhaps via its website.

- When they meet
- Where they meet
- The average duration of the meetings

- At what stage in the proceedings the talk takes place – for example, over breakfast, or after dinner
- How many people are likely to attend?
- The kind of people – and their particular interests – that generally come along
- The name, address and contact number(s) of the person who books speakers (often called the Programme Secretary).

Bear in mind that whilst local societies may be delighted to hear from an author direct, as it helps them to fill their programme, larger organisations may be more used to dealing with publishers and agents and find it easier that way. As one commented:

'I normally book authors through their publicists or agents, and it can be both difficult and unproductive if authors contact me direct. In truth, it tends to be the ones who are less well known and in whom I am least likely to be interested. Some of them are extremely persistent and have a totally unrealistic view of why they should be included and the kind of audience they will attract! It is much easier to say "no" politely to a publicist than to an author themselves.'

You have been warned.

What to send out to advertise your services

- A letter to the person who books speakers, introducing yourself and providing details of how to contact you
- An information sheet on your book (perhaps a copy of the advance notice – see Chapter 3 – or a leaflet produced by your publisher). Even if the talk you are offering is unrelated to your book, something proving that a book exists is a good idea
- A list of options as to what you could talk about (for an example, see below)
- Feedback from those who have heard you speak before. If you have a website and keep it up to date with testimonials, you could refer those who are interested in booking you to it.

Alternatively, keep a running sheet of quotations, all shown in inverted commas with the names and organisations they represent listed. Don't just put initials – it then sounds as though they are not real people. As to where to get such testimonials, remember that it is standard practice for programme secretaries to write after the event to thank you

- An indication of when you are available, in general terms. For example, if you have a regular teaching commitment one day of the week, say now, but don't go into a detailed description of your diary for the next three months. Bear in mind that there is often a long time period between sending information and being approached – one author told me recently of an 18-year wait!

Take your time before finalising what you send. Even though it's tempting to whack off an email immediately you hear of an organisation, think carefully about what kind of impression you want to create. Remember that your offer will most likely be discussed at a committee meeting; what you sent in will be passed around, so the more interesting/impressive the package, the more likely you are to be approached for a booking.

What you could offer

It is a good idea to draw up a short menu of options with which to tempt them. I would recommend including several items on the list, so that if the most obvious choice does not appeal, another on your list may be considered. Keep the wording short and snappy – if they do decide to use you, it will probably form the basis of the programme entry.

Getting paid for what you do: how to stick up for yourself without sounding strident

This is a tricky area. There seems to be an entirely unhelpful notion prevailing in society that true writers are not in it for the money, and that artists in general thrive on difficult financial

Alison Baverstock

I could talk about:

How to get a book published

If you feel you 'have a book in you', how should you go about getting it out? Which are the most sensible publishing houses to approach, and do you need an agent before you start? How likely are you to get accepted straightaway, and how do you keep your morale going – and keep writing – when you receive rejection letters? What does it feel like to see your name in print? I can offer first-hand, practical advice, having now had 14 books published.

How books are made

What happens in the making of a book, from the moment the manuscript is delivered to the appearance of final copies? How long does the whole process take, and who makes all the main decisions? Publishers refer to books that they turned down, but with which a rival house had great success, as 'the ones that got away'. So why was Harry Potter's true merit lost on so many houses? A fascinating insight into the world of publishing from someone who has worked in the industry for over 20 years.

How to set up a reading circle

Reading circles (or literary groups, as they are sometimes called) are the hottest trend in reading Britain – it was recently estimated that there are now over 30,000, and someone has just written a book on this (essentially Anglo-Saxon) phenomenon. So if you have longed to join a book circle, but not yet found one to join, why not set up your own?

I have now set up six reading circles, all of which are still running. What is the genesis of a good reading group? Supper or wine? Male, female or mixed company? Who should choose the books and how often should you meet?

All the above talks are adaptable for groups of children, with the addition of props and dressing up clothes.

10 Homersham Road, Kingston-upon-Thames, Surrey, KT1 3PN, UK
Telephone/Fax: +44 (0) 20 8546 2293   Mobile: 07765 934435   Email: alison.baverstock@btopenworld.com
Website: www.alisonbaverstock.com
VAT Registration No. 819 5836 88

circumstances; an appreciation of the garret as being the best environment for any form of creativity is hard to shift. I think, though, that as creative people we need to have our creativity acknowledged, and that the issue of payment should always be raised, even if it brings nothing more than an acknowledgement that whilst the organisation would like to pay, they unfortunately cannot.

> 'I came to this country on a musical scholarship from Australia, met my husband and have remained here ever since. When I was newly married my mother-in-law asked me to stand in at a service for the local (paid) organist who was ill. I agreed but asked them about the associated fee; this was tricky, although my forwardness was eventually notched up to my antipodean upbringing. But I stuck with it, waited patiently whilst the cheque book was taken out, the payee and amount were written and the cheque handed over – and then I handed it back to them. But I had made the point that they should pay for an artist's services, and it was one they did not forget – as some of them told me, years later.'
>
> Sally Mays, concert pianist

Some organisations will pay a fee; others offer travelling expenses; some may offer both. If the event includes a meal of some kind in a restaurant, you should not be expected to pay for yours.

Bear in mind too that whilst fees are often presented as fixed, in practice they may be negotiable. Travelling expenses can be particularly fluid, and sometimes made more generous so that they cover what amounts to a fee as well. The Society of Authors likes to insist that fees between speakers should be equal, whatever the type of book being written (children's writers used to be paid less) or the level of fame of the author. Indeed, if well-known authors stick out for a fee, which everyone else then gets, it helps all writers.

What level of fee to suggest is difficult. If you are speaking to a large audience from a multinational company, they will most likely be comfortable paying a vastly higher fee than a local primary school with absolutely no budget for such events. As a guideline, a useful figure to quote is the Society of Authors' recommended rate of £200 for half a day and £300 for a full day, and this is in line with levels of expenditure approved by regional arts boards. For a residency, week or a month, the Arts Council suggests that authors base their fee on an annual salary of £22,000. It certainly helps your case to mention that these authorities have suggested figures.

For workshops, you should certainly be paid – partly because this will require additional preparation, and partly because a more detailed and longer session with you may make the audience less likely to buy your book (they have already garnered all they need from you). If you were paid a one-off fee for writing your book, rather than royalties, you need a fee for this appearance (because the promotion will benefit others more than you). If no fee is available, your expenses should certainly be paid; find out how generous they are in establishing these.

However awkward, try to sort out your fee/expenses before the event, and put it in writing. Agree about what kind of expenses are chargeable; the usual practice is to charge for a second-class return rail fare, along with additional taxis and buses – and most organisations will require you to keep the receipts for reimbursement. Alternatively, you may be able to use your car at a certain amount per mile. If you have to stay overnight then accommodation may be offered at a committee member's house rather than the society having to incur a hotel bill. If you are offered such hospitality, do remember to write and thank your host – a failure to do so can be remembered long after your scintillating performance.

For taxation purposes, most authors will be self-employed and hence on Schedule D, in which case the organiser should not be deducting tax or NI contributions. Do discuss this early, as it can take ages sorting it out afterwards when the wrong amount has been deducted. Agree how long the payment period will be.

Book sales at events

Whether or not you get a fee, the opportunity to sell copies of your book should not be overlooked. This can be done at the end of the event, and it may help to encourage people to part with their money there and then if you offer a special discount to those present, and you offer to sign copies (take a decent pen with you). Your publisher may be willing to provide leaflets to hand out/ place on seats, and perhaps a showcard too (see chapter 3) to advertise the book and its price.

A good alternative option is to have your book included in the price of the entrance ticket, so each member of the audience gets a copy of the book to have signed and to go home with. You may have to give the organisers a substantial discount on the book's selling price to encourage this, but it is often popular with organisers as it represents very good value to the audience, and you sell many more copies than you would do otherwise.

When it comes to how the books get displayed, if you are lucky – if the audience is large, and sales of the books likely to be strong – the organisers may have been able to persuade a local bookseller to come along and attend, and sell stock (and you happily may end up 'in stock' with them too, if sales are good). Even if your publisher says they have told the bookseller, and the stock is on order, do ring and check that all is well with the bookseller. Not everything may be quite as well planned as it seems (because the publishers are dealing with lots of other authors asking for the same thing).

Alternatively, you could ask your publisher to produce some leaflets offering a special discount to those in the audience, which they redeem afterwards. For a conference or large speaking engagement, particularly one overseas, this is a much cheaper option than the publisher paying for books to be on a conference stand or leaflets formally inserted into delegates' packs, and so they may well assist you. Desk-top publishing machines mean it is vastly cheaper for them (or you, if you have the right software) to design and print off a quick flyer to promote your book.

If the publisher is sending stock to the event, be very meticulous in following up the detail. I have heard so many anguished stories of books being ordered from the publishers/ booksellers/wholesalers and then failing to arrive, that I really feel it's less stressful to do the organising yourself (although it's obviously tricky if you are going to travel by train).

If you are going to take stock of your book with you to sell, you need to negotiate a discount from your publisher, and agree who pays for carriage (usually the publisher if you order a reasonable quantity, say over 20). Some may give you a higher discount if you are selling copies for charity. And on the day, you also need to have someone in charge of selling/looking after your stock. Ask when you are making arrangements for the talk if someone could do this for you; it's quite embarrassing to be answering questions one minute and the next having to fumble for change – and you don't want to be put in the difficult position of stock going missing and as a result the event costing you money. Take along a receipt pad so that you can offer those who buy, proof of purchase – useful if the book is likely to be claimed as a business expense (other authors are very wise to this!).

Things to do before the day of the talk

- Find out about the group you are talking to. How long have they been in existence for; any famous founders or former members that you could refer to in your introduction?

- A bit of local knowledge goes down very well – so even if you are delivering a talk you have done many times before, try to customise what you say so it sounds as though it was prepared for the audience you address; make it personal. I find it is a good idea to start with a reference to something topical or of local application (the last time you were in this area; family connections with the area, etc.). If you get the chance, try to pick up a copy of the most recent local paper and flick through to find out what are current concerns/interesting topics in the area, or talk briefly to your host

- What is the average age of members? What kind of talks have gone down particularly well/bombed in the past? How many questions are there likely to be?

- Ask the person who books you to confirm all the details in writing beforehand. If they do not, write to them and confirm your understanding of what has been agreed. Ring a week beforehand to double-check. Not all voluntarily run societies are as efficient as you might hope. Date, time and location, and do you want to be met? Accommodation?

Walker Books, Waterstone's
and Nicola Morgan
invite you to the launch of

The Highwayman's Footsteps

by Nicola Morgan

Thursday 9th November, 6-8pm
Waterstone's,
West End of Princes Street, Edinburgh,
1st Floor - Children's Department

The Highwayman's Footsteps is a gripping historical
adventure, full of dramatic and dastardly deeds.
Suitable for all readers of 10 and over.
"Robert Louis Stevenson on caffeine …"
See www.nicolamorgan.co.uk for details

RSVP essential:
n@childliteracy.com

- What is the title of your session and how has it been announced? What is the title or theme of the larger event you are part of? Rather than just arriving and starting, I remember hearing politician Michael Foot make polite reference to the events before and after his at the Canterbury Festival; it went down very well

- Likely attendance and format of the event: hall or round table, microphones? And talking of technical equipment, will anyone check that this is working before the event?

- Ask who is going to introduce you, and if they need any more information about you in order to do an effective job. Ask them to phone you if they would like to talk to you in further detail. Find out if they have web access, and if so give them the address of your website so they can look up information on you and get it right. Ask if the person introducing you can mention that your book is available for purchase – in general, the more *you* mention it, the fewer will be the resulting sales

- Refreshments, and will you be joining in? Has anyone asked about your specific dietary requirements? A lot of people assume that vegetarians eat fish

- Handouts. Do they want you to provide one? Sometimes there are restrictions – for example, they are not allowed in the Edinburgh Book Festival because there is insufficient time between events to go in and pick up those that have been dropped on the floor

- Will you be recorded or podcast, and if so are you happy about this?

- Is anyone sponsoring the event? It's polite to say thanks

- What happens if the event gets cancelled? Do you still get your fee? How long beforehand is considered acceptable notice?

- Is any publicity planned? Will a photographer from the local press be present? If not, do you have time to set something up? Navigating the line between being a pushy person and a useful source of ideas is made more palatable for the organisers if they appreciate the benefits they will reap if an event goes well (better-known society with more members; more widely attended meetings in future; other good speakers willing to come and talk).

What to wear

Do think carefully about what to wear. There may be many in attendance, but there will only be one speaker, so don't imagine that nobody in the audience will notice. On the contrary, they will be considering your dress, whether or not they are conscious of doing so, for the duration of your talk. Try to match your outfit to the group in hand. For a formal evening event you need to know what the dress code is; for an afternoon discussion with an informal audience a more relaxed approach will be necessary. If, for political or social reasons, you decide to break a dress code (for example, UK Chancellor of the Exchequer Gordon Brown wearing a lounge suit rather than the more usual white tie to the annual – and usually highly formal – Mansion House dinner), it should be a deliberate decision rather than the result of failing to do your homework.

What to say

Think carefully about the format of your talk, and take advice from the Programme Secretary. How long should you talk for? Remember to allow plenty of time for questions, and if you think that these are going to be slow coming, suggest a couple to your contact in the organisation that they could perhaps ask themselves, to get things moving.

Bear in mind that different groups have very different dynamics, and that you will be catapulted into this – and expected to be flexible. For example, I gave a talk to a Working Parents Association recently. The evening began (rather surprisingly) with everyone introducing themselves on the basis of their name, their job and their childcare arrangements. I duly followed suit. I found that as I talked, the audience liked to comment on every point I made; each theme was discussed by those present (about 20) before moving onto the next one. Once I got used to this it was a pleasant way to proceed. I was able to get a feel for their sympathies and respond to them as I talked, and also did not have to do all the talking – although monitoring how far we should stray from the subject also fell to me.

What to take with you

You need very brief notes or headings on which you can expand. Never, ever, read a speech. As Michael Barratt, a hugely experienced television and radio presenter, put it:

> 'I still recommend those who are going to be addressing audiences regularly to try to develop the art of speaking ad lib. It's hard work. It means mentally rehearsing a logically progressive theme (not learning the actual words) over and over again until you have it clear-cut in the mind.
>
> The best way to do this, in my experience, is to write down five or six one-word "headlines" of the argument you want to pursue. See whether they make a sensible progression, building to a rational conclusion. Then commit them to memory. You may also like to write them down on a small card which can easily be referred to if memory fails when you're standing there and the mind goes completely blank.
>
> Developing this skill will have two main effects. It will help you to get across your message much more effectively by using conversational rather than written English. And it will gradually develop your confidence in changing tack when that vital "listening" process tells you it's necessary to do so.'
>
> *Making the Most of the Media*, Kogan Page

The talk

Props
If you can, try to take along some samples of what you are talking about. The editor who deals with arts and crafts titles for one

publisher routinely takes along pots to be handed round whilst she is talking. This makes points instantly comprehensible and is a lovely way of drawing the audience in.

Before you start, make sure you are standing comfortably (on both feet) and try to speak slowly – however slowly you think you are speaking, your audience could still probably benefit from you slowing down even more. Engage eye contact, and if you really are so nervous that the only way you can get through is by reading out what you have already prepared, make sure you look up at regular intervals. Public speaking really does get easier with practice. If you still feel terrified, consider taking an evening class in public speaking – or ask if you can take along a friend to 'interview' you for your talk, as this may seem less intimidating.

After your talk is finished, a note of thanks for an effectively organised evening is always appreciated. Thank your host for everything, and say that they are free to pass on your name to colleagues doing a similar job for other organisations. And prepare for the phone to ring ...

Summary of this chapter

Having got a booking to go somewhere and talk about your writing, it's tempting to leave it at that. But time spent in reconnaissance is seldom wasted. The more specific your talk to the group you address, the better your likely response. It's a good investment in your future writing.

15

How to organise a launch event

Authors often associate the publication of a book with a launch party. Although 20 years ago this was not uncommon, today launch parties are relatively rare. Financial realities have hit home and publishers have to be sure that a real benefit will accrue from the holding of a celebratory event on publication.

Such benefits could include:

* Press coverage. The right chemistry at a party (a mix of journalists and interesting people) can produce a complimentary feature in the media. This could include news coverage, mentions in gossip and diary columns, a feature in the trade press, which is read by booksellers, and so on
* An effective gathering can promote word-of-mouth recommendations about a book and encourage people to read it, particularly if those invited are inclined to talk
* Keeping the author and their agent happy. This can bring loyalty to the house and prolong the future relationship.

Whilst it doesn't follow that the lack of an offer of a party for your forthcoming book implies that there is no interest in it, you may decide to either help the publishers organise something (with them hopefully bearing the costs) or to organise something yourself. To follow are a few guidelines on how to run a successful event.

What kind of event?

The most common form of book launch is a pre-dinner drinks party, say from 6.30 to 8.00 p.m. Light snacks and drinks are provided, on the assumption that people will arrive around 6.45 to 7.00 p.m. and will be going on to eat somewhere else. A drinks party has the benefit of being fairly simple to organise. But as this is the most frequently held kind of event, you may decide that something different is more appropriate. For example, you could consider the following.

Breakfast

As breakfast is so often a hurried meal, or missed altogether, the chance to sit down and enjoy one in interesting company can be very appealing. For example, a local religious bookshop has started running regular breakfasts for the clergy on Friday mornings, a day that many clergy apparently have off. This offers them the chance to meet each other and hear about forthcoming products and offers. They find they get a very good take-up, and that a lot of business results.

A talk followed by lunch

To launch the Church of England's new liturgy, Common Worship, in November 2000, the designers Omnific staged an exhibition in the St Bride Printing Library, offered personal tours around it, and provided a finger buffet lunch (jointly hosted by Church House Publishing) afterwards.

A demonstration connected with the subject of your book, followed by refreshments

When promoting a book on the physicist Faraday, I once organised a demonstration of his most famous experiments in the lecture theatre where he first showed them to the world.

A stunt linked to your book

Catherine Charley embarked on a new series of factual books for Puffin – Extreme Expeditions:

> 'I arrived at Waterstones in the centre of Belfast on a sledge pulled by a team of six huskies! This all linked into the theme of one of the books, *The Big Freeze*, which is about expeditions in the Arctic and Antarctic. TV, radio and newspapers all turned up and there was some great publicity as a result.'

An event that has nothing to do with the book but is appealing to the market

Education Direct organised a presentation on their new database, 'Spirit', followed by a trip on the London Eye for all those who attended. This got a very good response.

Whatever the format you eventually decide on, it's vital to consider the following:

- What do you want out of it? Will the event you are planning permit this? For example, if it is crucial for you as the author to have an intimate chat with a particular journalist, then a party may not be the best way to achieve this. Would going out to lunch be more successful?

- How much time do the key people you want to attend have at their disposal? Unless your event is mind-blowingly arresting, it's most likely pointless to organise an all-day event if you are trying to get the attention of busy press people who have only half an hour at most to spare

- Is there a synergy between function and format? Breakfast is delicious but messy. Does it provide enough time and space for writing/interviewing, if this is integral to what you want to achieve?

- Do you feel comfortable with what is suggested? A hapless press event makes a better story for the media than one which runs smoothly, so do ensure that you can carry off whatever is suggested. For example, if you are a keen hiker, then climbing a mountain and handing a copy of your book on rural Wales to the press at the bottom may be very successful. If, however, despite immense knowledge of your subject, age these days prevents you from straying far from your car, you may end up looking ridiculous.

Where to hold your event?

There are probably lots of venues that have experience of hosting the kind of event you have in mind. Alternatively, rack your brain for some new inspiration! For example:

- Many local bookshops have room to stage an event. This has the advantage of fitting in with their own PR plans (i.e. they may help fund the event), and books, and the mechanisms for selling them, will be there already
- A local historic house or building (or its garden, depending on the time of year)
- A friend with a large house able to accommodate the event
- A local hotel (again, the manager may deem this good for PR and not charge you)
- A 'grunge' event. A completely unlikely location might attract media attention – perhaps a car park or a railway station waiting room (permission will be needed).

Wherever you decide on, find out about the practical details:

- Is access easy? If not, forget it
- Is the venue interesting? Has it been overused by similar events or is it innovative?
- What about parking?
- Do they have a licence to serve drink (i.e. it is there already), or do you have to bring your own?
- Are there enough loos for the assembled company?
- What about coats and umbrellas – where will they be put?
- What about glasses, cutlery and plates?
- Are there chairs for those who can't stand up?

When to hold your event

Timing is very important. You need to consider time of year, time of week, time of day.

- Avoid Friday and Saturday evenings – most people have their own plans
- Monday is a bad day if you want the Sunday press to attend; it is usually their journalists' day off

- Summer holidays – often known as 'the silly season', but a great time for attracting attention to an appropriate story

- Watch out for public holidays, paying particular attention to those you don't celebrate yourself – for example, Halloween (31st October), Burns Night (25th January). Either avoid them or tie your event in with the public occasion

- Avoid regular and scheduled mass media interest events. For example, US Presidential elections are always on the first Tuesday of November, every four years; the inauguration is two months later

- Do you want people to nip in after work or make an evening of it? If the latter, the chances are they will stay longer and drink more!

Whom to invite

- Representatives of the media (broadcast and print) likely to be interested. Find out the names of the relevant editors and ask them, and the features writers who write for them. Be sure to include the local media

- Celebrities who will add a buzz to the event

- Other high-profile people who have a connection with the subject-matter of the book

- Local booksellers

- Friends and relations (keep this list moderate – a group of loyal retainers adds atmosphere to an event for those just arriving, but you don't want it to look so much like a family reunion that others feel excluded). Do encourage your contacts to talk to people other than those they know already

- Those involved in the production of the book – freelance editors, proofreaders, illustrators, and so on. They are often forgotten and can be resentful.

How far ahead to invite?

Send your invitations too far ahead, and they risk getting lost; too close and those you invite may already be committed. About six weeks prior to the event is good. The invitation (preferably printed, so that it looks professional and easy to read) should include all the relevant details:

- Who is doing the inviting? (Company, individual or both – for example, the Managing Director and staff of ...)
- If there is a keynote speaker already in place, you may want to mention them on the invitation
- Title and publisher of what is being launched
- Venue
- Date
- Time
- Dress (casual/informal/formal/black tie)
- To whom should recipients reply, and how (email, telephone, address, etc.)
- A request for any other information you need prior to the event (for example, for security considerations do you need car registration numbers, etc.)?

Accompanying the invitation should be a press release (see chapter 10) giving further details of the project. This could include interesting information about the author, the book and the event/party being organised, where further information can be found, and how to get a review copy of the book.

Preparations before the event

Confirm all arrangements in writing with the venue; never rely on conversations to confirm the details. Hotels and formal venues will issue you with a contract, which does tend to concentrate the mind. Find out who will actually be running your event on the day: often this is not the person who took the booking from you.

Find out too what furniture is available to you. Are there enough tables on which to mount a display, and are table coverings available? If not, bring some (freshly ironed!) sheets. Then organise sustenance. In general, more white wine than red will be drunk, and do ensure that there are plenty of soft drinks – you will probably need more of these than you think. For a cocktail party offer food that can be eaten with the minimum of mess; avoid things that spurt butter or drip. Ask those handing food round to be methodical about approaching *everyone*: as a guest, it can be frustrating to see food drifting past and not be offered any. They don't need to interrupt a conversation to offer food – the arrival of a tray and the engagement of eye contact can be enough to provide the opportunity. Some hosts lay out a table of food and encourage guests to help themselves, but women in particular will find this awkward (they tend not to want to look hungry) and moving to the table can disrupt conversations.

If you are instructing caterers, you will need to confirm the numbers likely to attend a week before, and give a final head count 24 hours (or more) before the party starts. You will be charged per head on this figure, even if fewer than planned attend.

Ensure that there is someone on the door directing where coats should be put, and armed with a complete list of names of everyone attending; they should tick the names off as people arrive. Alternatively, ask people to sign a visitors' book so you capture their names and addresses for future use (mailing them information on your next book).

Do you plan to have name badges so that all present can see the names of those they talk to? If so, make the badges large enough to allow space for a size of text that is readable. Most people prefer ones that can be clipped to your clothes rather than requiring a pin (less risk of damage to the fabric).

Ask the publisher (in writing) for stock of the book well before the launch. This sounds obvious, but if you don't ask for them, they may get overlooked. Double check that the stock is on its way two weeks before. Bear in mind that many of those attending may see it as their right to walk away with a free copy of the book. Remember that the perceived value of a give-away is vastly out of proportion to the actual cost to the publisher – production costs may be no more than 10 per cent of the finished cost of the item. But if this is a problem (for example, if you have to pay for the books taken away, or the publisher does not wish them to be handed out and so erode the basic market), have someone guard them! An effective rule of thumb is that the better paid your invitee list, the more they will assume that they have the right to free goods: cardiologists and surgeons are notorious for taking advantage; teachers almost never do!

A speaker

Events to promote a book need a focus: someone needs to stand and say why everyone is gathered, and draw attention to key things about the project in question. Who should do the talk? I feel it's better for the author not to do it – it's difficult to deliver a panegyric yourself. But do reply.

Ask someone who people in attendance will be interested in meeting. They may do it for you, even if extremely busy, because:

- They like to be helpful
- The publicity will do them good
- They are keen to be associated with the project/cause you are promoting.

For your own contribution, there is useful guidance in the previous chapter of this book on public speaking, so I will be brief here. Make it relevant, witty, and avoid Oscar-style weeping, as demonstrated by Gwynneth Paltrow.

What those present should take away from such an event

Have a press pack available to the media. This is usually a folder including:

- A copy of the book
- A press release
- An author photograph (with a caption saying who it is and the name of the book on the back), and/or a link to a website offering a downloadable version
- Contact details (a telephone number, email address, website) in case they need more information whilst they are writing up
- Relevant information on other titles – for example, how well did the author's last title sell?
- The promotional plans for the title. This gives the journalist a sense of scale, i.e. how important this author is.

Offer everyone else the chance to buy the book. Either ask a local bookseller to come along and offer copies for sale, or order stock and get a friend to sell them for you. Ensure that they have a stock of change (most book prices end in 99p) and that cheques get signed! If you feel embarrassed about selling your books at your own party, then consider giving your royalty to charity, and having a sign up to that effect.

If the party is being held prior to the publication date, you will need to consult the publisher on whether sales can be made. You may be asked to refer sales to bookshops after publication instead.

Photographs

Will the publisher provide for the services of a freelance photographer to take pictures at the event? If not, is it worth arranging one yourself – or just equipping a friend with a camera?

Don't rely on photographers to know who/what you wish to be photographed. Brief them beforehand on what you want (relatively straightforward if they will recognise who they are meant to be photographing). Alternatively, send a friend or colleague who knows what you are looking for and get them to accompany the photographer around the room.

On the grounds that 'he who pays the piper calls the tune', ask that the photographer dresses appropriately. At a very smart event a photographer wearing jeans and a T-shirt will stand out like a sore thumb.

Follow-up after a launch event

Send photos, with captions, by email to the media who did not attend but seemed interested. Attach an accompanying press release saying how successful it was. Do you have any anecdotal feedback worth passing on? Can you provide some yourself? For example:

> 'It seems that prawn-lovers adore Catherine Jones's books. And they descended en masse on a book launch in Borders on Tuesday last. Within 5 minutes of arrival there were absolutely none left! The reason for this ...'.

Or:

> 'Beaujolais Nouveau hits Kingston. The Wilson Hall was packed last Friday as wine lovers eager to sample the new vintage stampeded into the first place in Surrey to have any. As you can see from the attached picture, daringly taken by our intrepid photographer ...'.

Why your publisher should bear the costs of a launch you have organised yourself

Publishers will hate me for this, but here are some points you could put to them:

- You have done all the organisation for them; thus they save staff time and effort
- Your organisation will cost a fraction of what it would have cost to get professional caterers to do it for them
- It's very good PR for their publishing house
- It's an excellent chance for them to display other titles from their range (you could offer their catalogues for display)

- If you invite representatives of the local book trade, it can promote relations with their key customers.

Case Study

An example of this in practice

My last book was the result of an event at the Edinburgh Book Festival. I gave a talk on what personal resources are needed by would-be writers, answered lots of questions – and then my two elder children and I went off to eat and see the comedian Russell Brand (in a show, not one-to-one). But I woke up the next morning in my hotel room with an exciting plan – it had suddenly struck me that the talk could be turned into a book. I hopped out of bed, drew back one of the curtains, and started writing a contents list. *Is there a book in you?* was brought back to the Edinburgh Festival as a published book in August 2006.

My children, who had been sharing a room with me at the time when inspiration struck, were less impressed, shouting at me to turn the light off (it was not on, the morning was just bright). But as the book had begun in a very specific location, with one of my favourite views in the world in front of me (over the city and out towards the Firth of Forth) and was being brought back as a finished book one year on, I thought it would be a great idea to have a party to celebrate. I contacted the hotel, The Bonham in Drumsheugh Gardens, and they were keen. The publishers were already doing a lot to support the book, and were hosting a launch for the centenary edition of the *Writers' & Artists' Yearbook* later the same week; they felt that if I wanted a separate launch that was fine, but it was up to me. I got support from The Bonham (who gave us the function room without charge, got their PR lady to send out the press releases, and agreed that we set a limit on cost), and I asked my employers at Kingston University if they would like to chip in too. They kindly said yes and we went ahead.

The result was a most enjoyable evening. We celebrated publication of the book, and along came many friends from the Edinburgh area: university friends (both my husband and I went to St Andrews); writers (I had given a talk to the Scottish Society of Authors earlier in the year); publishers; academics teaching Creative Writing and Publishing Studies; and booksellers, as well as some accompanying media. Our 11-year-old son sold the books, and as we were giving the royalties to a local children's hospice, most people forgave him his hard-sell tactics ('if you buy two you get *two* free pens'). I will probably not be able to work out if it was worth it financially, but from a personal point of view it felt tremendous. The picture shows the three people who were there when the whole thing began, one year on.

The Faculties of Business and Law, and Arts and Social Sciences
request the pleasure of your company at a reception to celebrate the publication of

Is there a book in you?

by Alison Baverstock

Tuesday 22nd August 2006
6.00pm - 8.00pm, The Bonham Hotel, 35 Drumsheugh Gardens
Edinburgh EH3 7RN

KINGSTON
UNIVERSITY

RSVP
Alison Baverstock
T: 020 8546 2293
E: a.baverstock@kingston.ac.uk

Summary of this chapter

Don't expect your publishers to lay on a party to mark publication. There are better ways for them to spend money, to ensure that your book gets noticed by the media and stocked in bookshops. Instead, consider organising your own. Having a book published is a great thing to celebrate, and you might even be able to persuade other people (your employer, the local bookshop or the publisher) to help with the costs.

16

Keeping up momentum and morale: before and after publication

For the writer preparing a book, the delivery date dominates for months ahead. And during the final weeks before delivery it is all-consuming; one can think of little else. But once the manuscript has been handed over, it is the publication date that takes over as the key date.

What happens on publication?

Publishers announce a title's publication date six to nine months in advance. This is the date on which the selling of stock may begin (although it is sometimes ignored to secure a competitive advantage). About three weeks before publication is the 'release date', when titles are sent out to bookshops in preparation for publication.

At about this time books are also sent out to review editors for them to commission reviews from their regular writers. When the reviews actually appear may vary – those for the last Harry Potter title appeared on publication day, and reviews for mass-market fiction may appear within a couple of weeks of publication. For academic titles, which are reviewed in irregularly published journals, the process may take months. For the fortunate, publication may be accompanied by requests for interviews, appearances in the broadcast media and local events, and perhaps a book-signing in a local store or an interview with the local paper. So if this is possible, do ensure that you are available – now is not the best time to take your long planned overland trekking trip to Nepal.

What do you do after publication?

With luck, you will already have embarked on your next writing job – indeed, it can be quite difficult at publication to focus on what is by now your previous book (so be sure to re-read it before any interviews take place). Now is also a good time to think about what to do next.

What is your long-term aim?

Particularly if this is your first book, this is a good time to think about your motivation. Adapting the French proverb about food, do you write to live or live to write? Or given the economics of writing, do you do neither; does some other activity subsidise your writing? How serious are you about your writing? Consider the following questions:

- How do you describe yourself on forms you have to fill in; at parties?
- How do your family describe you? Is it in the same terms as you would use yourself?
- Are you an author or a writer? I tend to think of authors as writing fiction, and writers as those who turn their hand to most things – for example, journalism.
- What professional associations or writers' groups do you belong to?

In the wider world ...

For me, having a book published was a personal pinnacle. It was something I had wanted to achieve for a very long time, and finally seeing my name in print was immensely satisfying. I cried. Not everyone sees it as quite so important:

- Car insurers are suspicious, often asking for special terms from writers
- Having had various jobs in the book trade, I have experimented with a range of titles on my name badge at the London Book Fair. The one that aroused least eye contact and most averted gazes was 'author'
- If you are successful, the most likely response from the community of writers will be resentment. As one person put it to me:

'No one minds real writing talent being acknowledged, but I find the complete randomness of fame as a writer and associated talent very depressing. Most writers are intensely jealous people.'

For the vast majority of writers, their work is under-rewarded and lonely. Here is another writer's view:

'When my first book came out, none of my family seemed quite sure how to react. My husband showed a copy to his parents. They could not have been less interested. My aunt (and godmother) has never mentioned it, although I know my mother has told her about it. None of them have read it. I think they were all rather worried about making me big-headed. The experience taught me a lesson; that what had been my whole life's ambition was in fact a very personal goal, and one that I could not expect anyone else to feel proud of, just for my sake.'

Another wrote to me after publication of *Is there a book in you?*:

'The only thing I felt was a little too sanguine was your chapter on personal support mechanisms. I have known cases where a deep-seated jealously has led one partner to disparage and actively hinder the writing ambitions of the other. Without being sexist, I feel that some men find it very hard to cope with a wife or female partner's success. Also parents and siblings can be very destructive about a family member who "presumes" to write.'

The highs of being a writer are undeniable – seeing your book for the first time, a satisfying review, a positive letter from a reader –

but they are also so utterly unrelated to the really relevant slog of just keeping going.

Building a support network

There will be some of your acquaintance, friends and family, who are silently (or not) just amazed that you have got published and feel you are in imminent danger of becoming far too big for your boots. Such people may have to be tolerated, but as they will do nothing to help your writing, or your sense of yourself as a writer, try to build a support network of people who are pleased, and who don't mind you ringing to complain about how difficult the writing bit is, or to relate the latest dispiriting conversation with your publisher without immediately needing to remind you that 'you are lucky to have one'. Such support networks often work best with others who are 'creatives' but are not in direct competition with you – perhaps writers of other types of material, actors or artists. And of course the real supporters are those who are just dead impressed that you are trying to write at all. The best way to prompt such support is to be an encourager yourself.

Keep your profile high

The very celebrated may bemoan the lack of privacy brought by success, but for the vast majority of writers a little recognition works wonders.

When running publicity campaigns, professionals will try to orchestrate an ongoing sequence of appearances, to build and maintain a profile, rather than a one-off hit at publication time. If you do not have the services of a publicity professional at your disposal to achieve this for you, how can you maintain your profile in between books?

- Aim for a variety of different appearances; don't do too many things at one time. Be selective
- Be consistent. A letter in a newspaper can be a very effective way of reminding people you are there, but the opposite effect is achieved if your name is always appearing
- Give talks on your subject matter. Giving a talk on a book you have written exposes you to your market, to those who find the

subject (or perhaps just the fact that you have written a book) fascinating. It's also a wonderful way of exploring your own argument; trying to explain a subject clearly to others is surely the best test of logic. Answering questions at the end of a talk forces you to reassess trends and examine what is going on right now; to have your own opinions challenged by those with an outlook you do not usually meet in your own social or professional circles. I confess that on such occasions I love the buzz; the reassertion of myself as a writer – and you may end up with an idea for a feature article connected with a topical aspect of your book (which, if accepted for publication, breathes new life into sales!)

- Wherever you go, take along leaflets on your books. If there are many, from several different publishers, think about producing a leaflet listing all the titles you have in print yourself, asking the various publishers involved to make a contribution – they may well agree, as it is cheaper than them bearing all the costs themselves, and will be handed straight to the likely purchasers

- Write an article for the trade or writing press

- Offer to review books in a publication you would like to be reviewed in yourself. If you have reviewed before, send in samples; if not, write a sample and send it in to illustrate your style. Find out the name of the reviews editor and send it in personally addressed. Remember that controversial opinions are more likely to get noticed, but that memories can be very long – be careful of compromising your own future 'reviewability'

- Write for a newsletter or house magazine – many organisations (public and private) produce them. Can you write a feature to be included (it may have to be for nothing, but always ensure that you get your 'byline' – including the title of your book, the publisher and your own website – or name at the end of the piece). Yearbooks often need relevant articles – can you be included here? As a guide to which ones to approach, start by thinking about those you use yourself on a regular basis, or looking in your local library

- Write articles for the press – local and national. Again, payment is not certain, but the byline is crucial

- Send information to a gossip column. Most professional magazines have 'people' sections, often passing on trade gossip or announcing promotions

- Send a photograph of your book or a book-related event to the media. Most of the photographs sent into such sections are very dull – lots of people lined up with a drink in their hand. So send a photograph (with a caption) with information on you or your book for inclusion. Ensure that the quality of the photograph sent (it must be digital) is of a sufficiently high resolution for it to be reproduced; the most common reason for rejecting photos is that they are not

- Become an after-dinner (or after-lunch) speaker. Lots of organisations need speakers – and it provides a very useful opportunity to sell copies of your book afterwards. Even better, can you get your book included in the admission price?

- Get your book adopted on a training course and perhaps included in the course price. Delegates love to go away with an 'added value' extra, and your publishers would probably sell at a hefty discount to any organisation taking a bulk order of at least 20 copies

- Send your CV to programmes on which you would like to be considered as a panellist. The producers on all these programmes have books of names and contact numbers for experts they can call on to contribute. So list your specialisation and give them proof that you can talk (a list of what else you have appeared on)

- Give guest lectures at local colleges and universities. There are now colleges running undergraduate and post-graduate courses in publishing worldwide, and many would welcome a talk from a writer on how it feels to be published

- Give time to a good cause or campaign that has a public profile. Get involved with one you really believe in and give it full support rather than dabbling in lots of different ones

- As you become better known, you too will be asked for endorsements. Be careful: apply your recommendation without sufficient thought and you risk devaluing your approval; endorse too many things and you can build up media resistance. Don't become a 'rent a quote'

- Try to stimulate your brain with new ideas. Watch programmes you don't usually see, read a different daily newspaper from your habitual one, go to places you don't usually visit and listen to what other people are saying. Try morning television and see who calls in, or go to a football match and listen. Learn from this. Such events widen your vocabulary and experience of life, and at the same time you may come across new markets for your books, new ways of selling them, as well as new ideas for books

- Go to exhibitions and galleries. I find wonderful thinking space here, which refreshes my imagination and gives me new ideas – sometimes from watching other people there, looking at the discount structures for admission or just the items for sale in the gift shop

- Volunteer your services for a judging panel. There are lots of literary competitions today, and all need judges who may or may not be remunerated. This keeps your name in the media, and can be a useful platform for freelance journalism, which again can improve book sales.

Reminders on this fame business

Being a full-time writer is a life of immense ups and downs. But whilst society loves to knock someone off their plinth – especially if you are seen to take yourself too seriously – a writer needs their ego. You need to carry on believing that what you have inside you is worth passing on to other people, and keep the determination to sustain you whilst writing and searching for a publisher.

But remember that society expects those who become famous also to be nice, and this can be difficult to keep up in public all the time – particularly if what motivated you to write a book was an old bitterness which the amateur psychiatrist, of which there are so many these days, reckons any sane person would have ditched long ago.

Some writers cope with this by developing a 'writing persona'. On the basis that people take you at your own estimation, they present a character that is interesting to the media and which can be sustained. They are outrageous, melancholic or flirtatious on demand; whatever their 'personality' is reckoned to require. This will be hard work, and may cause internal struggle as the image of the crying clown testifies, but at least as a performance art it can be relinquished on your return home.

The most dangerous thing is to start believing your own publicity. Just because the media is willing to record what you have to say, doesn't mean that you will always say what you mean, or even that they will broadcast what you say. And once you become well known, you never know who is watching you (although they will probably remember the encounter more than you):

'So XX deplores lack of manners in other people (Q&A, 23rd September)? Well, so do I, which is why I was not impressed when I sold her some cinema tickets a couple of years ago. She spent the entire transaction yakking on her mobile phone, neither acknowledging nor thanking me.'

Letters Page, *Weekend Guardian*, 30th September 2006

With this in mind, and to prepare all budding authors for stardom, I hope that the following piece from journalist and author Celia Brayfield[1], first published in *The Times*, will be helpful.

Spoilt by Stardom

Fame should not be a licence to behave boorishly.

Fame may be short but life will probably be long, and the successful celebrity knows that it ain't how you start, but how you finish that really counts. For the guidance of the newly famous, therefore, Miss Manners suggests the following:

---

1 www.celiabrayfield.com

1 Be nice, especially to your peers. The media will love it if you slag off your fellow artists, but the media don't run the business you are in.

2 Try not to act like a prat. Don't claim special privileges or advertise your limitations.

3 Keep in mind that you are not the only person on the planet.

4 Never, ever write an autobiography. Write a diary instead. Don't admit this until publishers beat down your door, then sit back and collect the royalties in your old age.

5 Have the right friends. The friends who offer to buy your drugs or stage your photo-opportunities will be the ones who shop you to the tabloids and pose for the paparazzi at your funeral.

6 Give back. Never forget that the public think you owe them. Their perception is that you are enjoying unattainable benefits that you don't deserve. Follow the example of Sting or JK Rowling: pick at least one charity and support it as visibly and as substantially as you can.

7 If possible, be witty.

8 Learn to say no. You will get more demands on your time, more begging letters and more long-lost rellies coming out of the woodwork than you could possibly imagine. Turn people down gracefully, or create a tsunami of resentment.

9 Remember, you didn't do it all yourself. You did of course. Nobody else wrote that book, played that part or scored that goal. But you've been inappropriately rewarded for it and you must make amends. So when you make your acceptance speech, thank everyone and keep them happy.

10 Sweat the small stuff. One of the myths of being famous is that you will have 'people' who'll take care of everything for you. Many of them take care of themselves first. Check your tax returns, read your balance sheets, get second opinions.

11 Learn the difference between attention and approval (see 1 above). Only do things that gain you approval. Brattish behaviour will only get you attention. Getting attention is not a worthwhile career unless you are two years old or under.

Index

Advance notice/information
   sheet 29
Agents
   approaching 42, 57–64, 75,
     76–85
   leaving 84–85
Amazon 190
Author etiquette 127–128
Author's publicity form 28,
   116–119
   talks 202, 208–220
   view of publishers 8–11

Blogs 171–174
   benefits of 173–174
   why write one? 171–172
   legal consideration 172
Blurbs 72–74
Books
   problems of selling 21
   purchasing 22
   stocking & buying 192–193
   value for money 24
Booksellers
   chains 181–182
   independents 182–183
   the trade 178–191
Bookselling 23
Bookshops 180–189
   events in 186–189
Brochures 34

Catalogues 32
Commissioning editors 88
Contacts 88
Cover blurb 32
CVs 67–69

Databases 28, 100–101
Direct marketing 36

Editor, role of 95–97
Egos 14–15
Endorsements 70–72

Feedback 43–45
Festivals 193–197

Introductory letters 59–64

Journalists 131–132, 137–138

Key accounts manager 34

Launches 221–233
   follow-up 230
   location 223–224
   preparation for 226–228
   press packs 228–229
   type 221–223
   when to hold 224–225, 226
   who to invite 225
Leaflets/flyers 35
Library events 197–197
Local press 141–142

Market, outline of 69–72
Marketing 1
   budgets 27
   definition 17
   how it works 26
Marketing/Sales directors 27,
   34
   marketing your own book
     92–93

meetings with publishers
  120–127
plans 27
relationships 20
spcific marketing 18
theory 16
Marketing potential 69
Media interviews 142–144
Merchandising 39
Money 77–78

Point of sale material 34
Press advertising 37
Presenters 34
Press releases 138–141
Professional organisations 89
Promotional copy 52–57
Promotions 38
Publication date and after
  235–242
Publicists 131
Publicity and PR 39
Publicity
  author involvement 132–135
  coverage 135–136
  how it's done 130–132
  timing 136–137
  what is it 129–130
Publishers
  approaching 42, 57, 86–90
  as communicators 9
  view of authors 12–14
  working with 114–116

Reading circles 201–202

Sales conferences 33
Self-publishing 91–113
  achieving publicity 99
  approaching the market
    97–99
  database management
    100–101
  getting reviews 97–99
  know your market 92
  order fulfillment 101
  publicity 137–138
  selling your own book 93–94
  talks 208–220
Show cards 35
Slush pile 89
Society of Authors 89
Submitting your manuscript 44,
  45, 46–50, 79–80
Synposis 65–67

Trade advertising 37

Websites 30, 153–177
  blogs 171–174
  costs 166–168
  designers 161–162
  getting people to use 168–171
  how they are used 154
  payments to 167–168
  reading & writing 191
  updating 162
  who sets it up? 158–166
  your own website 154–158
Writing groups & circles 44,
  205